Jesus the Christ

Jesus the Christ

A Bibliography

Leland Jennings White

Michael Glazier, Inc.
Wilmington, Delaware

BIOGRAPHICAL NOTE

Leland Jennings White is Professor of Theology and Culture at St. John's University, New York, and Editor of *Biblical Theology Bulletin*. Having earned an S.T. L. from the Gregorian University and a Ph.D. in Religion and Culture from Duke University, he has taught Christology in theologates in Seattle and Detroit, and in various summer graduate programs before writing *Christ and the Christian Movement, Jesus in the New Testament, the Creeds and Modern Theology* (1985). In 1986-87 he was awarded the Leo John Dehon Fellowship for Research on the relationship between Christology and Social Action.

First published in 1988 by Michael Glazier, Inc., 1935 West Fourth Street, Wilmington, Delaware 19805.
©1988 by Michael Glazier, Inc. All rights reserved.

Library of Congress Catalog Card Number: 88-45085
International Standard Book Number: 0-89453-645-1

Typography by Angela Meades.
Printed in the United States of America.

To my parents,
Leland S. and Winifred White,
who taught me to read
and showed me how to read between the lines
for meaning.

Contents

Part III:
New Testament Christology and Soteriology

Part IV. Christ in Historical Dogmatic Theology

Part V.
Contemporary Approaches and Issues in Christology

Please Note

- We invite our readers to submit to the author any corrections, suggestions, or additions to the bibliography.
- An asterisk before a title indicates that the work is of broad interest and serves as a good introduction to the topic.

Introduction
Study of Christ in the Church Today

Christology is the church's study of Jesus of Nazareth. Often enough this or that miscarriage of mission or ministry in the contemporary church is blamed on an inadequate or erroneous grasp of Christology. Understand who Christ is to understand what the church must be. This prescription is so common that we should be suspicious. The two decades of teaching, research and writing on Christology that lie behind this bibliography have persuaded me that the prescription has the right ingredients, but in the wrong order. Understanding the church, the concrete historical church comes first.

Before we can understand anything said about Jesus, we have to know the church from which the statement of faith comes. This should seem odd. Three out of the four gospel accounts of Christ were written without mention of the church. Indeed, Christ was a central theme of theology and preaching for fifteen hundred years when the church was barely mentioned in theological writings. Nonetheless, if Christ was the issue at Nicaea and Chalcedon, Vatican I and II focused on the church. In so doing, these recent councils reflect the introspective self-reflective course typical of everyday modern life. What book on Christ can we read today without asking *Whose Christ is this?* What gospel writers, theologians, pastors and other humans mean to say about Christ or anything else is, we now assume, embedded in that web of meaningful relationships we call their socio-religious world or church.

For those who need an explanation for contemporary human self-consciousness, a self-consciousness that makes even the churchly community reflect on itself even before it tries to deal with divine revelation, I offer one suggestion: the printed book. Books in standard form, readily available to large numbers of people, and read privately, opened up new worlds for believers. Before print believers primarily heard of and experienced Christ as though present in the spoken word or sacramental action. The world into which Christ came was the world they lived in, a world that might indeed be overshadowed by the world to come, but none-theless a unified whole of heaven and earth that all alike assumed to be the setting for understanding God, Christ and themselves. Books, and later radio, films and television invited us to imagine altogether other worlds, worlds quite different from our own. We inevitably compare one text with another—assessing continuities and discontinuities—and, we grasp the fact that some ground is strange, some manners alien, some meaning incommunicable.

However more complicted an explanation for modern self-consciousness about statements on Christ, or any other subject, may become, the books we read and write are clear evidence for the fact of ever-more absorbing concern with the question of where, when and why such statements are made. Only a couple of decades ago, for Catholics, and perhaps a century or more ago for other Christians, a bibliography on Christ might have been arranged around dogmatic issues or tracts. So standardized was the arrange-ment of questions from the medieval *summas* to the pre-Vatican II manuals that the dates and locations of their authors would appear superfluous, at least to the authors themselves.

But this is the salient point. Instinctively, we date such manuals. We judge that they come from a world curiously out of touch with the fact of history, a world in which propositions are taken as timeless truths. Even as a community of believers, we have become historically conscious, which means that we are conscious of how different our grasp of Jesus is from any other people of any other time and place—however much we may place ultimate trust in one and the same person. Before print and whatever other factors made us historically conscious, Jesus was studied in a community of believers who very largely thought the whole task was simply stating as clearly as possible who he was and what he had done for humanity. Since then, quite clearly, the task has been not so much clearly stating his identity as searching through the debris of history for that identity.

The search for the Jesus of History is both a distinct phase and an overarching symbol of post-print Christological concerns. The major portion of the works in this bibliography may be seen in terms of our efforts to reconstruct a Jesus uncontaminated by later church dogma. This was the necessary first stage. Christians came, as it were, to understand that the light created by the stained glass of dogmatic and sacramental tradition was if not wholly artificial, at least of human making. Hence, the determination to sift through the most ancient documents, removing the medieval and patristic filters. In this phase, we developed the sensitivity for methodical research into sources and language contained in Part I of the present bibliography. At the end of this search we knew that between us and the historical Jesus of Nazareth lies a stream of history never to be adequately crossed.

But this ending has also been a beginning. Gradually, a two-fold awareness has emerged from our search. First, having begun with the conviction that the church stood between us and Jesus, we came to recognize ever more clearly that we moderns—however much we may have tried to stand aside from the church of tradition—were yet ourselves part of that ever growing stream of believers shaping, reshaping, filtering and refiltering the historical reality of Jesus. Showing how the Constantinian church created icons of Christ reflecting imperial images, we were at first startled and discouraged to see ourselves in the pre-Constantinian layers we had uncovered. Part II of this bibliography shows both our commitment to the search and our growing realization of limited results.

The second level of awareness that has emerged from our search for the historical Jesus is an ever clearer individual and corporate self-awareness that takes the form of a genuine self-affirmation. The works in Parts III and IV of this bibliography show how the identity of Jesus as Christ and Saviour was envisioned by the New Testament writers and the later church. For the most part, the contemporary scholars who search these traditions appreciate two facts that emerged in the earlier quest. First, they are willing to acknowledge, and even to highlight, the distinctive genius of those who shaped the earlier visions, realizing that Jesus interpreted by a Paul, for example, is afterall more than a Jesus seen by the mythical naked eye of the scientific historian. Thus, second, they more easily accept the fact that their own is an interpretation, a way of envisioning Christ, in some real way a contribution rather than a mere repetition of fact.

Part V suggests the fruit of these developments in Christology. The study of Christ in the hands of scholars at various levels ever more capable of acknowledging their own capacity for reimagining the shape of their own lives, and the meaning of Jesus' life for their lives, increasingly moves towards issues of contemporary concern, to dismantle barriers between individuals and groups, to shape political life, to enlarge our cultural vision and to deepen our interpersonal life.

This collection of books, then, reveals not only much about its subject matter, in this case how God's involvement with us shows forth in Christ, but also, and perhaps more importantly, how we stand together as a community of believers in the church, a community of humans in the world. These books are less records of who Christ was than they are part of the communications network begun by Jesus of Nazareth to link us to one another, to make us understand one another at the depth we think possible only to God, and likely only to a divine person fully involved in human life.

Leland J. White
St. John's University
New York City

I. Foundations

1
Bibliographies and Bibliographical Studies

Edwards, Denis. *What Are They Saying About Salvation?* New York: Paulist Press, 1986.

Kissinger, Warren S. *The Lives of Jesus. A History and Bibliography.* New York: Garland Publishing Co., 1985.

_____ *The Parables of Jesus. A History of Interpretation and Bibliography.* Metuchen, NJ: Scarecrow Press/American Theological Library Association, 1979.

Mackey, James P. "Jesus in the New Testament. A Bibliographical Survey." *Horizons* 1 (1974, pp. 51-73).

Metzger, Bruce M., ed. *Index to Periodical Literature on Christ and the Gospels.* Grand Rapids, MI: Wm. B. Eerdmans Publishing Co., 1962.

O'Collins, Gerald. *What Are They Saying About the Resurrection?* New York: Paulist Press, 1978.

Richard, Lucien. *What Are They Saying About Christ and World Religions?* New York: Paulist Press, 1981.

Scroggs, Robin. "The Sociological Interpretation of the New Testament. The Present State of Research." *New Testament Studies* 26 (1979/80), pp. 164-179.

2
Methods, Models and Language

Barr, James. "Some Thoughts on Narrative, Myth and Incarnation." *God Incarnate. Story and Belief,* ed. by A.E. Harvey. London: SPCK, 1981, pp. 14-23.

Bultmann, Rudolf. *Jesus Christ and Mythology.* New York: Charles Scribner's Sons, 1958.

Congar, Yves. "Christ in the Economy of Salvation and in our Dogmatic Tracts." *Who Is Jesus of Nazareth?* ed. by E. Schillebeeckx et al. New York: Paulist Press, 1965, pp. 5-25.

Cupitt, Don. *The Debate About Christ.* London: SCM Press, 1979.

de Jonge, Marinus. *Jesus. Inspiring and Disturbing Presence.* Nashville, TN: Abingdon Press, 1974.

Frei, Hans W. *The Identity of Jesus Christ. The Hermeneutical Bases of Dogmatic Theology.* Philadelphia: Fortress Press, 1975.

Goulder, Michael, ed. *Incarnation and Myth. The Debate Continued.* Grand Rapids, MI: Wm. B. Eerdmans Publishing Co., 1979.

Green, Michael, ed. *The Truth of God Incarnate.* Grand Rapids, MI: Wm. B. Eerdmans Publishing Co, 1977.

(Response to Hick, *The Myth of God Incarnate* - editor's note).

Hick, John, ed. *The Myth of God Incarnate.* London: SCM Press, 1977.

Jones, Geraint Vaughan. *Christology and Myth in the New Testament. An Inquiry into the Character, Extent and Interpretation of the Mythological Element.* New York: Harper & Row, 1956.

Katz, Stephen T. "The Language and Logic of 'Mystery' in Christology." *Christ Faith and History* ed. by S. W. Sykes and J. P. Clayton. New York: Cambridge University Press, 1972, pp. 239-261.

Knox, John. *The Humanity and Divinity of Christ. A Study of Pattern in Christology.* Cambridge: Cambridge University Press, 1967.

Lash, Nicholas. "Son of God.' Reflections on a Metaphor." *Jesus, Son of God?* ed. by E. Schillebeeckx and J.-B. Metz. New York: The Seabury Press, 1982, pp. 11-16.

Rahner, Karl. "The Position of Christology in the Church Between Exegesis and Dogmatics." *Theological Investigations,* XI, trans. by D. Bourke. New York: Crossroad, 1982 reprint; first ET 1975, pp. 185-214.

_____ "The Two Basic Types of Christology." *Theological Investigations,* XIII, trans. by D. Bourke. New York: Crossroad, 1983 reprint; first ET 1975, pp. 213-223.

Riggin, George A. "Two Christic Paradigms. Focuses of a Theological Revolution." *Christological Perspectives,* ed. by R. F. Berkey and S. A. Edwards. New York: Pilgrim Press, 1982, pp. 238-260.

Yungblut, John R. *Rediscovering the Christ.* New York: The Seabury Press, 1974.

3
Survey Books and Articles

* Brown, Raymond E. "Who Do Men Say that I Am?—A Survey of Modern Scholarship on Gospel Christology." *Biblical Reflections on Crises Facing the Church.* New York: Paulist Press, 1975, pp. 20-37.

Chestnut, Glenn F. *Images of Christ. An Introduction to Christology.* Minneapolis, MN: The Seabury Press, 1984.

Dodd, C. H. *The Founder of Christianity.* New York: Macmillan, 1970.

* Duling, Dennis C. *Jesus Christ Through History.* New York: Harcourt Brace Jovanovich, Inc., 1979.

Dwyer, John C. *Son of Man & Son of God. A New Language for Faith.* New York: Paulist Press, 1983.

Grant, Frederick C. "Jesus Christ." *The Interpreter's Dictionary of the Bible,* ed. by G. A. Buttrick et al. Nashville, TN: Abingdon Press, 1962, Vol. 2, pp. 869-896.

Grillmeier, Alois. "Jesus Christ. III. Christology." *Sacramentum Mundi. An Encyclopedia of Theology,* ed. by K. Rahner et al. New York: Herder and Herder, 1969, vol. 3, pp. 186-192.

Grollenberg, Lucas. *Jesus.* John Bowden, trans. Philadelphia: The Westminster Press, 1978.

* Hart, Thomas N. *To Know and Follow Jesus. Contemporary Christology.* New York: Paulist Press, 1984.

* Hayes, John H. *Son of God to Superstar. Twentieth Century Interpretations of Jesus.* Nashville, TN: Abingdon, 1976.

McDermott, Brian. "Jesus Christ in Today's Faith and Theology." *Jesus, Son of God?,* ed. by E. Schillebeeckx and J.-B. Metz. New York: The Seabury Press, 1982, pp. 3-10.

McIntyre, John. *The Shape of Christology.* Philadelphia: The Westminster Press, 1966.

O'Grady, John F. *Models of Jesus.* Garden City, NY: Doubleday, 1981.

Rahner, Karl. "Jesus Christ. IV. History of Dogma and Theology." *Sacramentum Mundi. An Encyclopedia of Theology,* ed. by K. Rahner et al. New York: Herder & Herder, 1969, vol. 3, pp.192-209.

* White, Leland Jennings. *Christ and the Christian Movement. Jesus in the New Testament, the Creeds and Modern Theology.* New York: Alba House, 1985.

4
Multi-Author Collections and Festschrifts

Bammel, Ernst, ed. *The Trial of Jesus. Cambridge Studies in Honor of C. F. D. Moule.* Napierville, IL: Alec R. Allenson, Inc., 1970.

_____, and Moule, C. F. D., eds. *Jesus and the Politics of His Day.* New York: Cambridge University Press, 1984.

Bell, G. K. A., and Deissmann, D. A., eds. *Mysterium Christi.* London: Longmans, Green and Co., 1970.

Berkey, R. F., and Edwards, S. A., eds. *Christological Perspectives.* New York: Pilgrim Press, 1982.

Groh, Dennis E., and Jewett, Robert, eds. *The Living Text. Essays in Honor of Ernest W. Saunders.* Lanham, MD: University Press of America, 1985.

Harvey, Anthony E., ed. *God Incarnate. Story and Belief.* London: SPCK, 1981.

Lindars, Barnabas, and Smalley, Stephen S., eds. *Christ and Spirit in the New Testament. Essays in Honor of C. F. D. Moule.* Cambridge: Cambridge University Press, 1973.

McFadden, Thomas M., ed. *Does Jesus Make a Difference?* New York: The Seabury Press, 1974.

McKinney, R. W. A., ed. *Creation, Christ and Culture.* Edinburgh: T. & T. Clarke Ltd., 1976.

O'Donovan, Leo J., ed. *Word and Mystery. Biblical Essays on the Person and Mission of Christ.* Glen Rock, NJ: Newman Press, 1968.

Richardson, Peter, and Hurd, John C. eds. *From Jesus to Paul. Studies in Honor of Francis Wright Beare.* Waterloo, Ontario: Wilfred Laurier University Press, 1984.

Schillebeeckx, Edward, and Metz, J.-B., eds. *Jesus, Son of God?* New York: Seabury Press, 1982.

Schillebeeckx, Edward, et al. *Who Is Jesus of Nazareth?* New York: Paulist Press, 1965.

Schultz, Hans Jurgen, ed. *Jesus in His Time,* B. Watchorn, trans. Philadelphia: Fortress Press; 1971.

Sykes, S. W., and Clayton, J. P., eds. *Christ Faith and History. Cambridge Studies in Christology.* New York: Cambridge University Press, 1972.

Trotter, F. Thomas, ed. *Jesus and the Historian. Written in Honor of Ernest Cadman Colwell.* Philadelphia: The Westminster Press, 1968.

5
Official Church Statements

Dollen, C. J., McGowan, J. K., and Megivern, J. J., eds. *The Catholic Tradition. The Savior.* 2 Vols. Wilmington, NC: McGrath Publishing Co., 1979.

International Theological Commission. *Select Questions on Christology.* Washington: United States Catholic Conference, 1980.

—————— *Theology, Christology, Anthropology.* Washington: United States Catholic Conference, 1983.

Wadlington, Amanda G., ed. *Christ Our Lord. Official Catholic Teachings.* Wilmington, NC: McGrath Publishing Co., 1978. (Restricted to 20th century—Editor's Note)

6
Anthologies and Source Books

Carmody, James M., and Clarke, Thomas E., eds. *Word and Redeemer. Christology in the Fathers.* Glen Rock, NJ: Paulist Press, 1966.

Norris, Richard A., Jr., translator, editor. *The Christological Controversy.* Philadelphia: Fortress Press, 1980.

Sheets, John R., ed. *The Theology of the Atonement, Readings in Soteriology.* Englewood Cliffs, NJ: Prentice-Hall, Inc., 1967.

Tapia, Ralph J., ed. *The Theology of Christ.* New York: Bruce, 1971.

II. Jesus In Historical Perspective

7

General Approaches to
the Historical Jesus

Anderson, Hugh. *Jesus and Christian Origins. A Commentary on Modern Viewpoints.* New York: Oxford University Press, 1964.

Betz, O. *What Do We Know About Jesus?* Philadelphia: The Westminster Press, 1968.

* Cook, Michael L. *The Historical Jesus. Guidelines for Contemporary Catholics.* Chicago: The Thomas More Press, 1986.

Dahl, Nils Alstrup. *Jesus in the Memory of the Early Church.* Minneapolis: Augsburg Publishing House, 1976.

_____ "The Problem of the Historical Jesus." *The Crucified Messiah and Other Essays.* Minneapolis: Augsburg Publishing House, 1974, pp. 48-89.

De Rosa, Peter. *Jesus Who Became Christ.* Denville, NJ: Dimension, 1974.

Gogarten, Friedrich. *Christ the Crisis. Basic Questions Concerning Christology.* R.A. Wilson, trans. Richmond: John Knox Press, 1970; first ed. 1967.

Harvey, Anthony E. "Christology and the Evidence of the New Testament." *God Incarnate. Story and Belief,* ed. by A. E. Harvey. London: SPCK, 1981, pp. 42-54.

Leon-Dufour, Xavier. *The Gospels and the Jesus of History,* J. McHugh, trans. New York: Desclee Co., 1968.

Marrow, Stanley B. *The Words of Jesus in Our Gospels. A Catholic Response to Fundamentalism.* New York: Paulist Press, 1979.

* McArthur, Harvey K. *The Quest Through the Centuries.* Philadelphia: Fortress Press, 1966.

Nolan, Albert. *Jesus Before Christianity.* Maryknoll, NY: Orbis Books, 1978.

Pcsch, Rudolf. "Jesus Christ. II. Quest of the Historical Jesus." *Sacramentum Mundi: An Encyclopedia of Theology,* ed. by K. Rahner et al. New York: Herder & Herder, 1969, vol. 3, pp. 183-186.

Rahner, Karl. "Remarks on the Importance of the History of Jesus for Catholic Dogmatics." *Theological Investigations, XIII,* trans. by D. Bourke. New York: Crossroad, 1983 reprint; first ET 1975, pp. 201-212.

Ramsey, Michael. *Jesus and the Living Past.* New York: Oxford University Press, 1980.

8
The "The Life of Jesus" Movement

Grant, Robert H. *The Earliest Lives of Jesus*. New York: Harper & Brothers, 1961.

Herrmann, Wilhelm. *The Communion of the Christian with God*. R. T. Voelkel, ed. Philadelphia: Fortress Press, 1971 reprint; first ET 1906.

* Kissinger, Warren S. *The Lives of Jesus. A History and Bibliography*. New York: Garland Publishing Co., 1985.

Loisey, Alfred. *The Gospel and the Church*. Introduction by B. B. Scott. C. Home, trans. Philadelphia: Fortress Press, 1976 reprint; first ET 1903.

Massey, Marilyn Chapin. *Christ Unmasked. The Meaning of "The Life of Jesus" in German Politics*. Chapel Hill, NC: University of North Carolina Press, 1983.

Pals, Daniel L. *The Victorian "Lives" of Jesus*. San Antonio, TX: Trinity University Press, 1982.

Renan, Ernest. *The Life of Jesus*. Introduction by John Haynes Holmes. New York: Modern Library, 1927; orig. ed. 1863.

Schleiermacher, Friedrich. *The Life of Jesus*. S. M. Gilmour, trans., J. C. Vergeyden, ed. Philadelphia: Fortress Press, 1975 reprint; first ed. 1832.

Talbert, Charles H., ed. *Reimarus. Fragments.* R. S. Fraser, trans. Chico, CA: Scholars Press, 1985 reprint; Philadelphia: Fortress Press, 1970.

Weiss, Johannes. *The Kingdom of God.* R. H. Hiers and D. L. Holland, trans. Philadelphia: Fortress Press, 1971; orig. ed. 1892.

9
The Quest for the Historical Jesus

Anderson, Charles C. *Critical Quests of Jesus.* Grand Rapids, MI: Wm. B. Ecrdmans, 1969.

──────── *The Historical Jesus. A Continuing Quest.* Grand Rapids, MI: Wm. B. Eerdmans, 1972.

Barrett, C. K. *Jesus and the Gospel Tradition.* London: SPCK, 1967.

Braun, H. *Jesus of Nazareth. The Man and His Time.* Philadelphia: Fortress Press, 1979.

Bultmann, Rudolf. "The Primitive Christian Kerygma and the Historical Jesus." *The Historical Jesus and the Kerygmatic Christ,* ed. by C. E. Braaten & R. A. Harrisville. Nashville, TN: Abingdon, 1964, pp. 15-42.

Case, Shirley Jackson. *Jesus. A New Biography.* New York: Greenwood Press, 1968 reprint; original edition, 1927.

Craig, William Lane. *The Historical Argument for the Resurrection of Jesus during the Deist Controversy.* Lewiston, NY: The Edwin Mellen Press, 1985.

Dibelius, Martin. *Jesus.* Charles B. Hedrick and Frederick C. Grant, trans. Philadelphia: Westminster, 1949.

Kahler, Martin. *The So-Called Historical Jesus and the Historic Biblical Christ.* Carl E. Braaten, trans. Philadelphia: Fortress Press, 1964.

McArthur, Harvey K. *In Search of the Historical Jesus.* New York: Charles Scribner's Sons, 1969.

Mussner, Franz. *The Historical Jesus in the Gospel of John.* New York: Herder & Herder, 1967.

Nineham, D. E., et al. *Historicity and Chronology in the New Testament.* London: SPCK, 1965.

Peter, James. *Finding the Historical Jesus. A Statement of the Principles Involved.* New York: Harper & Row, 1965.

Schweitzer, Albert. *The Quest of the Historical Jesus. A Critical Study of its Progress from Reimarus to Wrede.* W. Montgomery, trans. New York: Macmillan Co., 1968.

Stauffer, E. *Jesus and His Story.* New York: Knopf, 1960.

Strauss, David Friedrich. *The Christ of Faith and the Jesus of History. A Critique of Schleiermacher's Life of Jesus.* Leander E. Keck, trans. ed. Philadelphia: Fortress Press, 1977; first ed. 1865.

_____ *The Life of Jesus Critically Examined.* P. C. Hodgson, ed., G. Elliott, trans. Philadelphia: Fortress Press, 1972.

Titus, Eric Lane. "The Fourth Gospel and the Historical Jesus." *Jesus and the Historian,* ed. by F. T. Trotter. Philadelphia: The Westminster Press, 1968, pp. 98-113.

Wrede, William. *The Messianic Secret.* J. G. Grieg, trans. Greenwood, SC: Attic Press, 1971, orig. ed. 1901.

* Zahrnt, H. *The Historical Jesus.* New York: Harper & Row, 1963.

10
The "New Quest" for
the Historical Jesus

Bornkamm, Gunther. *Jesus of Nazareth.* I. & F. McLuskey, trans. New York: Harper & Row, 1960.

* Braaten, Carl and Harrisville, Roy A., eds. *The Historical Jesus and the Kerygmatic Christ. Essays on the New Quest for the Historical Jesus.* Nashville, TN: Abingdon Press, 1964.

Conzelmann, Hans. *Jesus.* J. R. Lloyd, trans. Philadelphia: Fortress Press, 1973; first ed. 1959.

Fuchs, Ernst. *Studies of the Historical Jesus.* London: SCM Press, 1963.

Hahn, Ferdinand, Lohff, W., and Bornkamm. G. *What Can We Know About Jesus? Essays on the New Quest.* Philadelphia: Fortress Press, 1969.

Kasemann, Ernest. "Blind Alleys in the 'Jesus of History' Controversy." *New Testament Questions of Today,* trans. by W. J. Montague. Philadelphia: Fortress Press, 1969, pp. 23-65.

Robinson, James M. *A New Quest of the Historical Jesus and Other Essays.* Philadelphia: Fortress Press, 1983.

11
Jesus Research

Aulen, Gustaf. *Jesus in Contemporary Historical Research.* I. H. Hjelm, trans. Philadelphia: Fortress Press, 1976.

Buchannan, George Wesley. *Jesus. The King and His Kingdom.* Macon, GA: Mercer University Press, 1984.

Dahl, Nils Alstrup. "The Crucified Messiah." *The Crucified Messiah and Other Essays.* Minneapolis: Augsburg Publishing House, 1974, pp. 10-36.

Dunn, James D. G. *The Evidence for Jesus.* Philadelphia: The Westminster Press, 1985.

Fuller, Reginald H. "The Criterion of Dissimilarity." *Christological Perspectives,* ed. by R. F. Berkey & S. A. Edwards. New York: Pilgrim Press, 1982, pp. 42-48.

Harvey. A. E. *Jesus and the Constraints of History.* Philadelphia: The Westminster Press, 1982.

Hollenbach, Paul W. "Recent Historical Jesus Studies and the Social Sciences." *SBL Seminar Papers 1983.* Chico, CA: Scholars Press, 1983, pp. 61-78.

Jeremias, Joachim. *The Problem of the Historical Jesus.* Norman Perrin, trans. Philadelphia: Fortress Press, 1964.

_____ *Unknown Sayings of Jesus.* 2nd Ed. R. H. Fuller, trans. New York: Macmillan, 1964.

Keck, Leander E. *A Future for the Historical Jesus. The Place of Jesus in Preaching and Theology.* Philadelphia: Fortress Press, 1981; first ed. 1971.

Meyer, Ben F. *The Aims of Jesus.* London: SCM Press, 1979.

Trocme, Etienne. *Jesus as Seen by His Contemporaries.* Philadelphia: The Westminster Press, 1973.

12
Jesus' Cultural Setting: Social Historical Studies

Barrett, C.K. *The New Testament Background: Selected Documents.* New York: Harper & Row, 1961.

Bouquet, A. C. *Everyday Life in New Testament Times.* New York: Charles Scribner's Sons, 1953.

Fisher, Loren R. "Can This Be the Son of David?" *Jesus and the Historians,* ed. by F. T. Trotter. Philadelphia: The Westminster Press, 1968, pp. 97 ff.

Foerster, S. L. *From the Exile to Christ.* Philadelphia: Fortress Press, 1964.

Freyne, S. *Galilee from Alexander the Great to Hadrian.* Wilmington, DE and Notre Dame, IN: Michael Glazier and University of Notre Dame Press, 1980.

* _____ *The World of the New Testament.* Wilmington, DE: Michael Glazier, 1980.

Grant, Frederick C. *The Economic Background of the Gospels.* London: Oxford University Press, 1926.

Hengel, Martin. *Judaism and Hellenism. Studies in their Encounter in Palestine during the Early Hellenistic Period.* 2 Volumes. Philadelphia: Fortress Press, 1974.

Horsley, Richard A. *Jesus and the Spiral of Violence. Popular Jewish Resistance in Roman Palestine.* San Francisco, CA: Harper & Row, 1987.

Jeremias, Joachim. *Jerusalem in the Time of Jesus.* F. H. and C. H. Cave, trans. Philadelphia: Fortress Press, 1969.

Johnson, Sherman E. *Jesus in His Homeland.* New York: Charles Scribner's Sons, 1957.

Lohse, E. *The New Testament Environment.* Nashville, TN: Abingdon Press, 1976.

Norr, Dieter. "Problems of Legal History in the Gospels." *Jesus in His Time.* ed. by H. J. Schultz. Philadelphia: Fortress Press, 1971, pp. 115-123.

Reicke, Bo. "Galilee and Judaea." *Jesus in His Time,* ed. by H. J. Schultz. Philadelphia: Fortress Press, 1971, pp. 28-35.

_____ *The New Testament Era.* Philadelphia: Fortress Press, 1968.

Safrai, S. and Stern, M., et al., eds. *The Jewish People in the First Century. Historical Geography, Political History, Social, Cultural and Religious Life and Institutions.* Philadelphia: Fortress Press, 1974-76.

* Schultz, Hans Jurgen, ed. *Jesus in His Time.* B. Watchorn; trans. Philadelphia: Fortress Press, 1971.

* Schurer, Emil. *The History of the Jewish People in the Age of Jesus Christ (175 BC - AD 135).* 2 Volumes. Geza Vermes et al., eds. Edinburgh: T. and T. Clark, 1973-1979.

* Stambaugh, John E. and Balch, David L. *The New Testament in its Social Environment.* Philadelphia: Westminster Press, 1987.

13
Jesus' Cultural Setting: Social Science Studies

Derrett, J. Duncan M. *Jesus' Audience. The Social and Psychological Environment in which He Worked.* New York: The Seabury Press, 1974.

* Finley, M. I. *The Ancient Economy.* Berkeley: University of California Press, 1973.

Hollenbach, Paul W. "Recent Historical Jesus Studies and the Social Sciences." *SBL Seminar Papers 1983.* Chico, CA: Scholars Press, 1983, pp. 61-78.

Horsley, Richard A. and Hanson, John S. *Bandits, Prophets, and Messiahs. Popular Movements in the Time of Jesus.* Minneapolis: Winston Press, 1985.

* Malina, Bruce J. *Christian Origins and Cultural Anthropology. Practical Models for Biblical Interpretation.* Atlanta: John Knox Press, 1986.

* _____ *The New Testament World.* Insights from Cultural Anthropology. Atlanta: John Knox Press, 1981.

_____ "Jesus as Charismatic Leader?" *Biblical Theology Bulletin* 14 (1984), pp. 55-62.

Scroggs, Robin. 'The Sociological Interpretation of the New Testament. The Present State of Research.' *New Testament Studies* 26 (1979/80), pp. 164-179.

Sherwin-White, A. N. *Roman Society and Roman Law in the New Testament.* Oxford: Clarendon Press, 1963.

Vogtle, Anton. "The Miracles of Jesus Against their Contemporary Background." *Jesus in His Time,* ed. by H. J. Schultz. Philadelphia: Fortress Press, 1971, pp. 96-105.

14
Jesus' Cultural Setting: Literary Studies

Bailey, Kenneth E. *Poet and Peasant, and, Through Peasant Eyes. A Literary-Cultural Approach to the Parables of Luke* (Combined Edition). Grand Rapids, MI: Wm. B. Eerdmans Publishing Co., 1983.

Collins, John J. *The Apocalyptic Imagination. An Introduction to the Jewish Matrix of Christianity.* New York: Crossroad, 1984.

Hanson, Paul D. *The Dawn of Apocalyptic.* Philadelphia: Fortress Press, 1979.

* McNamara, Martin. *Intertestamental Literature.* Wilmington, DE: Michael Glazier, 1983.

* _____ *Palestinian Judaism and the New Testament.* Wilmington, DE: Michael Glazier, 1983.

Rowley, H. H. *The Relevance of Apocalyptic.* New York: Harper & Row, 1955.

Russell, David Syme. *Between the Testaments.* Revised Edition. Philadelphia: Fortress Press, 1965.

15
Jesus: The Jew

Aquinas, Thomas. *Summa Theologiae,* III, 40, 4.

Aron, Robert. *The Jewish Jesus.* Maryknoll, NY: Orbis Books, 1982.

Banks, R. *Jesus and the Law in the Synoptic Tradition.* New York: Cambridge University Press, 1975.

Barth, Markus. *Jesus the Jew.* F. Prussner, trans. Atlanta: John Knox Press, 1978.

Booth, Roger P. *Jesus and the Laws of Purity. Tradition History and Legal History in Mark 7.* Sheffield, England: JSOT Press, 1986.

Bowker, John. *Jesus and the Pharisees.* Cambridge: Cambridge University Press, 1973.

Charlesworth, James H. *Jesus Within Judaism.* Garden City, NY: Doubleday, 1987.

Cook, Michael L. "Jesus and the Pharisees—The Problem as It Stands Today." *Journal of Ecumenical Studies* 15 (1978), pp. 441-460.

Falk, Harvey. *Jesus the Pharisee. A New Look at the Jewishness of Jesus.* New York: Paulist Press, 1985.

Finkel, Asher. *The Pharisees and the Teacher of Nazareth.* Leiden: E. J. Brill, 1974.

Lambrecht, Jan. "Jesus and the Law: An Investigation of Mark 7:1-23." *Ephemerides Theologicae Lovanienses* 53 (1977), pp. 24-79.

McEleney, Neil J. "Authenticating Criteria and Mark 7:1-23." *Catholic Biblical Quarterly* 34 (1972), pp. 431-460.

Moo, D.J. "Jesus and the Authority of the Law." *Journal for the Study of the New Testament* 20 (1984), pp. 3-49.

Parkes, J. *Jesus, Paul and the Jews.* London: SCM, 1936.

Phipps, William E. "Jesus, the Prophetic Pharisee." *Journal of Ecumenical Studies* 14 (1977), pp. 17-31.

Riches, John. *Jesus and the Transformation of Judaism.* New York: The Seabury Press, 1982.

* Sanders, E. P. *Jesus and Judaism.* Philadelphia: Fortress Press, 1985.

* Tambasco, Anthony. *In the Days of Jesus. The Jewish Background and Unique Teaching of Jesus.* New York: Paulist Press, 1983.

Westerholm, S. *Jesus and Scribal Authority.* Lund: Gleerup, 1978.

16
Jesus: Birth

Aquinas, Thomas. *Summa Theologiae,* III, 28-33.

Boslooper, Thomas. *The Virgin Birth.* Philadelphia: The Westminster Press, 1962.

Bourke, Myles M. "The Literary Genus of Matthew 1-2." *Catholic Biblical Quarterly* 22 (1960), pp. 160-175.

Brown, Raymond E. *An Adult Christ at Christmas. Essays on the Three Biblical Christmas Stories.* Collegeville, MN: Liturgical Press, 1977.

* _____ *The Birth of the Messiah. A Commentary on the Infancy Narratives in Matthew and Luke.* Garden City, NY: Doubleday, 1977.

* _____ "The Problem of the Virginal Conception of Jesus." *The Virginal Conception and Bodily Resurrection of Jesus.* New York: Paulist Press, 1973, pp. 21-68.

_____ "Virgin Birth." *The Interpreter's Dictionary of the Bible,* ed. by Keith Crim et al. Nashville, TN: Abingdon, 1973, Supp Vol., pp. 940-941.

Campenhausen, Hans von. *The Virgin Birth in the Theology of the Ancient Church.* Napierville, IL: Alec R. Allenson Inc., 1964.

de Jonge, H.J. "Sonship, Wisdom, Infancy: Luke ii. 41-51a." *New Testament Studies* 24 (1978), pp. 317-354.

Enslin, Morton Scott. "The Christmas Stories of the Nativity." *Journal of Biblical Literature* 59 (1940), pp. 317-338.

Faris, Stephen. *The Hymns of Luke's Infancy Narratives. Their Origin, Meaning and Significance.* Sheffield, England: JSOT Press, 1985.

Fitzmyer, Joseph A. "The Virginal Conception of Jesus in the New Testament." *Theological Studies* 34 (1973), pp. 541-575.

Machen, J. Gresham. *The Virgin Birth of Christ.* Grand Rapids, MI: Baker House, 1945 reprint; first ed., 1930.

Mann, C. S. "The Historicity of the Birth Narratives." *Historicity and Chronology in the New Testament,* D.E. Nineham et al. London: SPCK, 1965, pp. 46-58.

Mather, F. Boyd. "The Search for the Living Text of the Lukan Infancy Narratives." *The Living Text,* ed. by D. E. Groh & R. Jewett. Lanham, MD: University Press of America, 1985, pp. 123-140.

Rahner, Karl. "Human Aspects of the Birth of Christ." *Theological Investigations,* XIII, trans. by D. Bourke. New York: Crossroad, 1983 reprint; first ET 1975, pp., 189-194.

—————— "Virginitas in Partu." *Theological Investigations,* IV, trans by K. Smyth. New York: Crossroad, 1982 reprint; first ET 1966, pp. 189-194.

Saliba, J.A. "The Virgin-Birth Debate in Anthropological Literature: A Critical Assessment." *Theological Studies* 36 (1975), pp. 428-454.

Stanley, David M. "St. Luke's Infancy Narrative." *Word and Mystery,* ed. by Leo J. O'Donovan. Glen Rock, NJ: Newman Press, 1968, pp. 143-154.

Winter, P. "Jewish Folklore in the Matthean Birth Story." *The Hibbert Journal* 53 (1954), pp. 34-42.

17

Jesus: Teachings

Aalen, Sverre. "'Reign' and 'House' in the Kingdom of God in the Gospels." *New Testament Studies* 8 (1962), pp. 215-240.

Baird, J. Arthur. *The Justice of God in the Teachings of Jesus.* Philadelphia: The Westminster Press, 1963.

—————— *Rediscovering the Power of the Gospel. Jesus' Theology of the Kingdom.* Wooster, OH: Iona Press, 1982.

Borg, Marcus J. *Conflict, Holiness and Politics in the Teachings of Jesus.* Lewiston, NY: The Edwin Mellen Press, 1984.

Bruce, F. F. *The Hard Sayings of Jesus.* Downers Grove, IL: Inter-Varsity Press, 1983.

Bultmann, Rudolf. *Jesus and the Word.* L. P. Smith and E. H. Lantero, trans. New York: Charles Scribner's Sons, 1958; first ed. 1926.

Chilton, Bruce D. *A Galilean Rabbi and His Bible. Jesus' Use of the Interpreted Scripture of His Time.* Wilmington, DE: Michael Glazier, 1984.

Crossan, John Dominic. *In Fragments. The Aphorisms of Jesus.* San Francisco: Harper & Row, 1983.

Davies, W. D. *The Sermon on the Mount.* Cambridge: Cambridge University Press, 1966.

Dodd, C. H. "Jesus as Teacher and Prophet." *Mysterium Christi,* ed. by G. K. A. Bell & D. A. Deissmann. London: Longmans, Green and Co., 1970, pp. 53-66.

Enslin, Morton Scott. *The Prophet from Nazareth.* New York: McGraw-Hill Book Co., Inc., 1961.

Farmer, William R. "Teaching of Jesus." *The Interpreter's Dictionary of the Bible,* ed. by Keith Crim et al. Nashville, TN: Abingdon, 1976, Supp. Vol., pp. 863-868.

Fuller, Reginald H. *The Mission and Achievement of Jesus. An Examination of the Presuppositions of New Testament Theology.* London: SCM Press, 1954.

Goergen, Donald J. *The Mission and Ministry of Jesus.* Wilmington, DE: Michael Glazier, 1986.

Hammerton-Kelly, Robert. *God the Father. Theology and Patriarchy in the Teaching of Jesus.* Philadelphia: Fortress Press, 1979.

Hunter, Archibald M. *The Work and Words of Jesus.* Revised Edition. Philadelphia: The Westminster Press, 1973.

Jeremias, Joachim. *New Testament Theology. The Proclamation of Jesus.* John Bowden, trans. New York: Charles Scribner's Sons, 1971.

Manson, T. W. *The Sayings of Jesus.* Grand Rapids, MI: Wm. B. Eerdmans Publishing Co., 1979.

_____ *The Servant-Messiah. A Study of the Public Ministry of Jesus.* New York: Cambridge University Press, 1953.

_____ *The Teachings of Jesus. Studies of its Form and Content.* New York: Cambridge University Press, 1963; first ed. 1931.

Otto, Rudolf. *The Kingdom of God and the Son of Man.* F. V. Filson and B. L. Wolff, trans. London: Lutterworth, 1938.

Perrin, Norman. *Rediscovering the Teaching of Jesus.* New York: Harper & Row, 1967.

Robbins, Vernon K. *Jesus the Teacher: A Socio-Rhetorical Interpretation of Mark.* Philadelphia: Fortress Press, 1984.

Scobie, Charles H. H. "Jesus or Paul? The Origin of the Universal Mission of the Christian Church." *From Jesus to Paul,* ed. by P. Richardson & J. C. Hurd. Waterloo, Ontario: Wilfred Laurier University Press, 1984, pp. 47-60.

Scott, Bernard Brandon. *Jesus. Symbol-Maker for the Kingdom.* Philadelphia: Fortress Press, 1981.

Stein, Robert H. *The Method and Message of Jesus' Teachings.* Philadelphia: The Westminster Press, 1978.

Trueblood, Elton. *The Humor of Christ.* New York: Harper & Row, 1964.

18
Jesus: Parables

* Boucher, Madeleine. *The Parables.* Wilmington, DE: Michael Glazier, 1981.

Carlston, Charles E. *The Parables of the Triple Tradition.* Philadelphia: Fortress Press, 1975.

Crossan, John Dominic. *In Parables. The Challenge of the Historical Jesus.* New York: Harper & Row, 1973.

Dodd, C. H. *The Parables of the Kingdom.* Revised Edition. New York: Charles Scribner's Sons, 1961; first ed. 1935.

Jeremias, Joachim. *The Parables of Jesus.* 2nd Revised Edition. New York: Charles Scribner's Sons, 1972.

* Kissinger, W. S. *The Parables of Jesus. A History of Interpretation and Bibliography.* Mctuchen, NJ: Scarecrow Press/American Theological Library Association, 1979.

Lambrecht, Jan. *Once More Astonished. The Parables of Jesus.* New York: Crossroad, 1981.

Linnemann, Eta. *Jesus of the Parables.* John Sturdy, trans. New York: Harper & Row, 1966.

Robinson, James M. "Jesus' Parables as God Happening." *Jesus and the Historian,* ed. by F. T. Trotter. Philadelphia: The Westminster Press, 1968, pp. 134-150.

Tolbert, Mary Ann. *Perspectives on the Parables. An Approach to Multiple Interpretations.* Philadelphia: Fortress Press, 1979.

Via, Dan Otto, Jr. *The Parables. Their Literary and Existential Dimensions.* Philadelphia: Fortress Press, 1967.

19
Jesus: Ethics and Eschatology

Furnish, Victor Paul. *The Love Command in the New Testament*. Nashville, TN: Abingdon Press, 1972.

Hiers, Richard H. *Jesus and Ethics. Four Interpretations*. Philadelphia: The Westminster Press, 1968.

_____ *Jesus and the Future. Unresolved Questions for Eschatology*. Atlanta: John Knox Press, 1981.

_____ *The Historical Jesus and the Kingdom of God. Present and Future in the Message and Ministry of Jesus*. Gainesville, FL: University of Florida Press, 1973.

* Jewett, Robert. *Jesus Against the Rapture. Seven Unexpected Prophecies*. Philadelphia: The Westminster Press, 1979.

Minear, Paul S. *Commands of Christ*. Nashville, TN: Abingdon Press, 1972.

Piper, J. *"Love Your Enemies." Jesus' Love Command in the Synoptic Gospels and the Early Christian Paraenesis*. Cambridge: Cambridge University Press, 1979.

* Sanders, Jack T. *Ethics in the New Testament. Change and Development*. Philadelphia: Fortress Press, 1975.

Wilder, Amos. *Ethics and Eschatology in the Teaching of Jesus*. Revised Edition. New York: Harper, 1950.

20
Jesus: Religious Attitudes

Aquinas, Thomas. *Summa Theologiae,* III, 21.

Dunn, James D. G. *Jesus and the Spirit. A Study of the Religious and Charismatic Experience of Jesus and the First Christians in the New Testament.* Philadelphia: The Westminster Press, 1975.

Guillet, Jacques. *The Religious Experience of Jesus and His Disciples.* St. Meinrad, IN: Abbey Press, 1975.

Howard, G. E. "Notes and Observations on the 'Faith of Christ'." *Harvard Theological Review* 60 (1967), pp. 459-465.

Jeremias, Joachim. *The Prayers of Jesus.* Napierville, IL: Alec R. Allenson Inc., 1967.

* Mackey, James P. "The Faith of the Historical Jesus." *Horizons* 3 (1976), pp. 155-174.

Michaels, J. Ramsey. *Servant and Son. Jesus in Parable and Gospel.* Atlanta: John Knox Press, 1981.

21
Jesus: Trial and Death

Bammel, Ernst, ed. *The Trial of Jesus. Cambridge Studies in Honor of C. F. D. Moule.* Napierville, IL: Alec R. Allenson Inc., 1970.

_____ "The Titulus." *Jesus and the Politics of His Day,* ed. by E. Bammel & C. F. D. Moule. New York: Cambridge University Press, 1984, pp. 353-364.

_____ "The Trial before Pilate." *Jesus and the Politics of His Day,* ed. by E. Bammel & C. F. D. Moule. New York: Cambridge University Press, 1984, pp. 415-451.

Benoit, Pierre. "Jesus Before the Sanhedrin." *Jesus and the Gospel, vol. 1,* trans. by B. Weatherhead. London: Darton, Longman & Todd, 1973, pp. 146-166.

_____ "The Trial of Jesus." *Jesus and the Gospel, vol. 1,* trans. by B. Weatherhead. London: Darton, Longman & Todd, 1973, pp. 123-146.

Blinzler, Josef. *The Trial of Jesus. The Jewish and Roman Proceedings Described and Assessed from the Oldest Accounts.* I. & F. McHugh, trans. Westminster, MD: Newman Press, 1959.

Catchpole, David R. "Trial of Jesus." *The Interpreter's Dictionary of the Bible,* ed. by Keith Crim et al.

Nashville, TN: Abingdon, 1976, Supp. Vol., pp. 916-919.

——————— *The Trial of Jesus. A Study in the Gospels and Jewish Historiography from 1770 to the Present Day.* Leiden: E. J. Brill, 1971.

——————— "The Triumphal Entry." *Jesus and the Politics of His Day,* ed. by E. Bammel & C. F. D. Moule. New York: Cambridge University Press, 1984, pp. 319-334.

Charlesworth, James H. "Jesus and Jehohanan. An Archaeological Note on Crucifixion." *Expository Times* 84 (1973), pp. 147-150.

Cohn, Haim H. *The Trial and Death of Jesus.* New York: Harper & Row, 1971.

Donhue, John R. "Passion Narrative." *The Interpreter's Dictionary of the Bible,* ed. by Keith Crim et al. Nashville, TN: Abingdon, 1976, Supp. Vol., pp. 643-645.

Fitzmyer, Joseph A. "Crucifixion in Ancient Palestine, Qumran Literature, and the New Testament." *To Advance the Gospel. New Testament Studies.* New York: Crossroad, 1981, pp. 125-146.

* Hengel, Martin. *Crucifixion in the Ancient World and the Folly of the Message of the Cross.* Philadelphia: Fortress Press, 1977.

Kelber, Werner H. *The Passion in Mark. Studies on Mark 14-16.* Philadelphia: Fortress Press, 1976.

Lampe, G. W. H. "The Trial of Jesus in the Acta Pilati." *Jesus and the Politics of His Day,* ed. by E. Bammel & C. F. D. Moule. New York: Cambridge University Press, 1984, pp. 173-182.

Lohse, Eduard. *History of the Suffering and Death of Jesus.* Martin O. Dietrich, trans. Philadelphia: Fortress Press, 1967.

O'Collins, Gerald. "Jesus' Concept of his own Death." *The Way* 18 (1978), pp. 212-223.

Schneider, Gerhard. "The Political Charge Against Jesus (Luke 23:2)." *Jesus and the Politics of His Day,* ed. by E. Bammel & C.F.D. Moule. New York: Cambridge University Press, 1984, pp. 403-414.

* Senior, Donald. *The Passion of Jesus in the Gospel of Mark.* Wilmington, DE: Michael Glazier, 1984.

* _____. *The Passion of Jesus in the Gospel of Matthew.* Wilmington, DE: Michael Glazier, 1985.

Sherwin-White, A. N. "The Trial of Christ." *Historicity and Chronology in the New Testament.* D. E. Nineham et al. London: SPCK, 1965, pp. 97-116.

* Sloyan, Gerard S. *Jesus on Trial. The Development of the Passion Narratives and Their Historical and Ecumenical Implications.* Philadelphia: Fortress Press, 1973.

Wilson, William R. *The Execution of Jesus.* New York: Charles Scribner's Sons, 1970.

Winter, Paul. *On the Trial of Jesus.* Berlin: Walter de Gruyter, 1961.

22
Jesus in Jewish Scholarship

* Ben-Chiron, Shalom. "The Image of Jesus In Modern Judaism." *Journal of Ecumenical Studies* 11 (1974), pp. 401-430.

Borowitz, Eugene B. *Contemporary Christologies. A Jewish Response.* New York: Paulist Press, 1980.

Buber, Martin. *Two Types of Faith.* N. P. Goldhawk, trans. New York: Harper & Row, 1951.

Catchpole, David R. *The Trial of Jesus. A Study in the Gospels and Jewish Historiography from 1770 to the Present Day.* Leiden: E. J. Brill, 1971.

Cornfeld, Gaalyah, ed. *The Historical Jesus. A Scholarly View of the Man and his World.* New York: Macmillan, 1982.

Flusser, David. *Jesus.* Ronald Walls, trans. New York: Herder & Herder, 1969.

Klausner, Joseph. *Jesus of Nazareth. His Life, Times and Teaching.* Boston: Beacon Press. 1964 reprint; first ed. 1925.

Lapide, Pinchas. *Israelis, Jews and Jesus.* P. Heinegg, trans. Garden City, NY: Doubleday, 1979.

_____ *The Resurrection of Jesus. A Jewish Perspective.* Introduction by C. E. Braaten. Minneapolis: Augsburg Publishing House, 1983.

_____, and Luz, Ulrich. *Jesus in Two Perspectives. A Jewish-Christian Dialog.* L. W. Denef, trans. Minneapolis: Augsburg Publishing House, 1985.

Montefiore, Claude G. *Some Elements of the Religious Teachings of Jesus.* London: Macmillan and Co., 1910.

Sandmel, Samuel. *We Jews and Jesus.* New York: Oxford University Press, 1965.

Vermes, Geza. *Jesus the Jew. A Historian's Reading of the Gospel.* New York: Macmillan Publishing Co., 1973.

_____ *Jesus and the World of Judaism.* Philadelphia: Fortress Press, 1983.

_____ "The Gospels Without Christology." *God Incarnate. Story and Belief,* ed. by A. E. Harvey. London: SPCK, 1981, pp. 55-68.

Walker, Thomas. *Jewish Views of Jesus.* New York: Arno Press, Inc., 1973 reprint; first ed., 1931.

Zeitlin, Solomon. *Who Crucified Jesus?* New York: Bloch Publishing Co. 1964 (5th ed.).

23
Jesus in Non-Canonical Traditions

Brownlee, William H. "Jesus and Qumran." *Jesus and the Historian,* ed. by F. T. Trotter. Philadelphia: The Westminster Press, 1968, pp. 52-81.

——————— "Messianic Motifs of Qumran and the New Testament." *New Testament Studies* 3 (1956/57), pp. 12-30; 195-210.

Bruce, F. F. *Jesus and Christian Origins Outside the New Testament.* Grand Rapids, MI: Wm. B. Eerdmans, 1974.

Carmignac, Jean. *Christ and the Teacher of Righteousness. The Evidence of the Dead Sea Scrolls.* Baltimore: Helicon Press, 1962.

Grant, Robert M., with Freedman, David Noel. *The Secret Sayings of Jesus. With an English Translation of the Gospel of Thomas by William R. Schoedel.* Garden City, NY: Doubleday & Co., 1960.

Stauffer, Ethelbert. *Jesus and the Wilderness Community at Qumran.* H. Spalteholz, trans. Philadelphia: Fortress Press, 1964.

Summers, Ray. *The Secret Sayings of the Living Jesus. Studies in the Coptic Gospel according to Thomas.* Waco, TX: Word Books, 1968.

Wenham, D. *The Jesus Tradition Outside the Gospels (Gospel Perspectives 5).* Sheffield, England: JSOT Press, 1984.

III. New Testament Christology and Soteriology

24
Person of Christ in the New Testament: General

Beare, F. W. *The Earliest Records of Jesus.* Nashville, TN: Abingdon, 1962.

Benoit, Pierre. "The Divinity of Jesus in the Synoptic Gospels." *Jesus and the Gospel. vol. 1,* trans. by B. Weatherhead. London: Darton, Longman & Todd, 1973, pp. 47-70.

Betz, Hans Dieter, ed. *Christology and a Modern Pilgrimage: A Discussion with Norman Perrin.* Missoula, MT: Scholars Press, 1974.

Bowman, J. W. *Which Jesus?* Philadelphia: Westminster Press, 1970.

Braun, Herbert. "The Meaning of New Testament Christology." *God and Christ. Journal for Church and Society. No. 5,* ed. by R. W. Funk. New York: Harper, 1968, pp. 89-127.

Craddock, Fred B. *The Pre-Existence of Christ in the New Testament.* Nashville, TN: Abingdon, 1968.

* Cullmann, Oscar. *The Christology of the New Testament. Revised Edition.* S. C. Guthrie and C. A. M. Hall, trans. Philadelphia: The Westminster Press, 1963, first ed. 1957.

Fiorenza, E. S. "Wisdom Mythology and the Christological Hymns of the New Testament." *Aspects of Wisdom in Judaism and Early Christianity,* ed. by R. Wilken.

Notre Dame, IN: University of Notre Dame Press, 1975, pp. 17-41.

Fitzmyer, Joseph A. *A Christological Catechism. New Testament Answers.* New York: Paulist Press, 1982.

* Fuller, Reginald H. *The Foundations of New Testament Christology.* New York: Charles Scribner's Sons, 1965.

Hammerton-Kelly, R. G. *Pre-Existence. Wisdom and the Son of Man. A Study of the Idea of Pre-Existence in the New Testament.* London: Cambridge University Press, 1973.

Hooker, Morna D. "Christology and Methodology." *New Testament Studies* 17 (1971), pp. 480-487.

Hurtado, Larry W. "New Testament Christology: A Critique of Bousset's Influence. *Theological Studies* 40 (1979), pp. 306-317.

Lampe, G. W. H. "The Holy Spirit and the Person of Christ." *Christ Faith and History,* ed. by S. W. Sykes and J. P. Clayton. New York: Cambridge University Press, 1972, pp. 111-130.

Leon-Dufour, Xavier. "Jesus Christ." *Dictionary of Biblical Theology, 2nd Ed.,* ed. by X. Leon-Dufour, trans. by P. J. Cahill & E. M. Stewart. New York: The Seabury Press, 1973, pp. 265-272.

Longenecker, Richard N. *The Christology of Early Jewish Christianity.* Napierville, IL: Alec R. Allenson Inc., 1970.

Maisch, Ingrid and Vogtle, Anton. "Jesus Christ. I. Biblical." *Sacramentum Mundi: An Encyclopedia of Theology,* ed. by K. Rahner et al. New York: Herder & Herder, 1969, pp. 174-183.

* Marxsen, Willi. *The Beginnings of Christology. A Study in its Problems.* Paul Achtemeier, trans. Philadelphia: Fortress Press, 1969.

_____. "Christology in the New Testament." *Interpreter's Dictionary of the Bible, Supp. Vol.,* ed. by Keith Crim et al. Nashville, TN: Abingdon, 1976, pp. 146-156.

Moule, C. F. D. *The Origin of Christology.* New York: Cambridge University Press, 1977.

Neil, Stephen. *Jesus through Many Eyes. Introduction to the Theology of the New Testament.* Philadelphia: Fortress Press, 1976.

Neyrey, Jerome H. *Christ Is Community. The Christologies of the New Testament.* Wilmington, DE: Michael Glazier, 1985.

O'Donovan, Leo J., ed. *Word and Mystery: Biblical Essays on the Person and Mystery of Christ.* Glen Rock, NJ: Newman Press, 1968.

Perrin, Norman. *A Modern Pilgrimage in New Testament Christology. Philadelphia: Fortress Press, 1974.*

Robinson, James M. and Koester, Helmut. *Trajectories Through Early Christianity.* Philadelphia: Fortress Press, 1971.

Sanders, Jack T. *The New Testament Christological Hymns. Their Historical Religious Background.* London: Cambridge University Press, 1971.

Schweizer, Eduard. *Jesus.* David E. Green, trans. Richmond: John Knox Press, 1971.

Stanton, G. N. "The Gospel Traditions and Early Christological Reflection." *Christ Faith and History,* ed. by S. W. Sykes and J. P. Clayton. New York: Cambridge University Press, 1972, pp. 191-204.

Taylor, Vincent. *The Person of Christ in New Testament Teaching.* New York: St. Martin's Press, 1958.

* Vawter, Bruce. *This Man Jesus. An Essay Toward a New Testament Christology.* Garden City, NY: Doubleday & Co., 1973.

25
Person of Christ
in the New Testament: Synoptics

Best, E. *The Temptation and the Passion. The Markan Soteriology.* New York: Cambridge University Press, 1965.

* Burrows, Millar. *Jesus in the First Three Gospels.* Nashville, TN: Abingdon, 1977.

Donahue, John R. "Temple, Trial and Royal Christology (Mark 14:53-65)." *The Passion in Mark. Studies on Mark 14-16,* ed. by W. H. Kelber. Philadelphia: Fortress Press, 1976, pp. 61-79.

Gaston, Lloyd. "The Messiah of Israel as Teacher of the Gentiles: The Setting of Matthew's Christology." *Interpretation* 29 (1975), pp. 29-40.

Gruenler, Royce Gordon. *New Approaches to Jesus and the Gospels: A Phenomenological and Exegetical Study of Synoptic Christology.* Grand Rapids, MI: Baker House, 1982.

* Kealy, Sean. *Who is Jesus of Nazareth? The Challenge of Mark's Gospel for Contemporary Man.* Denville, NJ: Dimension Books, 1977.

Kelber, Werner H. *Mark's Story of Jesus.* Philadelphia: Fortress Press, 1979.

Kingsbury, Jack Dean. *Matthew. Structure, Christology.* Philadelphia: Fortress Press, 1971.

_____. *The Christology of Mark's Gospel.* Philadelphia: Fortress Press, 1983.

_____. "The Composition and Christology of Mt 28:16-20." *Journal of Biblical Literature* 93 (1974), pp. 575-584.

Matera, Frank J. *The Kingship of Jesus. Composition and Theology in Mark 15.* Chico, CA: Scholars Press, 1982.

Moule, C. F. D. "The Christology of Acts." *Studies in Luke-Acts,* ed. by Leander Keck and J. Louis Martyn. Nashville, TN: Abingdon, 1966, pp. 171 ff.

* Reumann, John. *Jesus in the Church's Gospels. Modern Scholarship and the Earliest Sources.* Philadelphia: Fortress Press, 1968.

Stanley, David M. "Christ as Savior in the Primitive Christian Preaching." *Word and Mystery,* ed. by Leo J. O'Donovan. Glen Rock, NJ: Newman Press, 1968, pp. 21-46.

_____. "Christ as Savior in the Synoptic Gospels." *Word and Mystery,* ed. by Leo J. O'Donovan. Glen Rock, NJ: Newman Press, 1968, pp. 47-67.

Stanton, G. N. *Jesus of Nazareth in New Testament Preaching.* New York: Cambridge University Press, 1974.

Styler, G. M. "Stages in Christology in the Synoptic Gospels." *New Testament Studies* 10 (1964), pp. 398-409.

Suggs, Jack M. *Wisdom, Christology and Law in Matthew's Gospel.* Cambridge, MA: Harvard University Press, 1970.

Tannehill, R. "The Gospel of Mark as Narrative Christology." *Perspectives on Mark's Gospel (Semeia 16),* ed. by N. R. Petersen. Missoula, MT: Scholars Press, 1980, pp. 57-95.

26
Person of Christ in the New Testament: John

Boismard, M. E. "Jesus the Savior According to Saint John." *Word and Mystery,* ed. by Leo J. O'Donovan. Glen Rock, NJ: Newman Press, 1968, pp. 69-85.

* McArthur, Harvey E. "Christological Perspectives in the Predicates of the Johannine Ego Eimi Sayings." *Christological Perspectives,* ed. by R. F. Berkey & S. A. Edwards. New York: Pilgrim Press, 1982, pp. 79-94.

Meeks, Wayne A. *The Prophet-King. Moses Traditions and the Johannine Christology.* Leiden: E.J. Brill, 1967.

Minear, Paul S. "Logos Ecclesiology in John's Gospel." *Christological Perspectives,* ed. by R. F. Berkey & S. A. Edwards. New York: Pilgrim Press, 1982, pp. 95-111.

Roth, Wolfgang. "Jesus as the Son of Man: The Scriptural Identity of the Johannine Image." *The Living Text,* ed. by D. E. Groh & R. Jewett. Lanham, MD: University Press of America, 1985, pp. 11-26.

Thompson, Marianne Meye. *The Humanity of Jesus in the Fourth Gospel.* Philadelphia, PA: Fortress Press, 1988.

27
Person of Christ in the
New Testament: Paul

Ahern, Barnabas Mary. "The Contemporaneity of Christ's Passion in the Epistles of Saint Paul." *The Language of the Cross,* ed. by A. Lacomara. Chicago: Franciscan Herald Press, 1977, pp. 131-149.

Bossman, David M. *"In Isaac": A Midrashic Approach to Paul's "In Christ."* Ann Arbor, MI: University Microfilms, 1973.

Carrez, Maurice. "The Pauline Hermeneutics of the Resurrection." *The Resurrection and Modern Biblical Thought,* ed. by P. de Surgy et al. New York: Corpus Books, 1970, pp. 30-48.

* Cerfaux, Lucien. *Christ in the Theology of St. Paul.* G. Webb and A. Walker, trans. New York: Herder & Herder, 1959.

* Dahl, Nils Alstrup. "The Messiahship of Jesus in Paul." *The Crucified Messiah and Other Essays.* Minneapolis, MN: Augsburg Publishing House, 1974, pp. 37-74.

Dungan, David L. *The Sayings of Jesus in the Churches of Paul: The Use of the Synoptic Tradition in the Regulation of Early Church Life.* Oxford: Basil Blackwell, 1971.

Durwell, F. X. "Christ the Cosmic Lord in the Pauline Epistles." *A Companion to Paul. Readings in Pauline Theology,* ed. by M. J. Taylor. New York: Alba House, 1975, pp. 237-245.

* Fitzmyer, Joseph A. "Pauline Soteriology." *The Jerome Biblical Commentary,* ed. by R.E. Brown & J.A. Fitzmyer. Englewood Cliffs, NJ: Prentice-Hall, Inc., 1968, vol. II, pp. 805-817.

Hurd, John C. "The Jesus Whom Paul Preaches." *From Jesus to Paul,* ed. by P. Richardson & J. C. Hurd. Waterloo, Ontario: Wilfred Laurier University Press, 1984, pp. 73-89.

Hurtado, L. W. "Jesus as Lordly Example in Philippians 2:5-11." *From Jesus to Paul,* ed. by P. Richardson & J.C. Hurd. Waterloo, Ontario: Wilfred Laurier University Press, 1984, pp. 113-126.

Lambrecht, J. "Paul's Christological Use of Scripture in 1 Cor 15, 20-28." *New Testament Studies 28* (1982), pp. 502-527.

Lyonnet, Stanislaus. "The Return of Christ to God According to St. Paul." *Word and Mystery,* ed. by Leo J. O'Donovan. Glen Rock, NJ: Newman Press, 1968, pp. 201-229.

Murphy-O'Connor, Jerome. "Paul's Understanding of Christ as the Personal Presence of God in the World." *A Companion to Paul. Readings in Pauline Theology,* ed. by M. J. Taylor. New York: Alba House, 1975, pp. 1-12.

Ridderbos, Herman. *Paul and Jesus. Origin and General Character of Paul's Preaching of Christ.* D.H. Freeman, trans. Grand Rapids, MI: Baker, 1958.

Rollins, Wayne G. "Christological *Tendenz* in Colossians 1:15-20: A Theologia Crucis." *Christological Perspectives,* ed. by R. F. Berkey & S. A. Edwards. New York: Pilgrim Press, 1982, pp. 123-138.

Roy, Leon. "Reconciliation." *Dictionary of Biblical Theology,* 2nd. Ed., ed. by X. Leon-Dufour, trans. by P.J. Cahill. New York: The Seabury Press, 1973, pp. 479-480.

Segal, Alan F. "'He Who Did Not Spare His Own Son...'—Jesus, Paul and the Akedah." *From Jesus to Paul,* ed. by P. Richardson & J.C. Hurd. Waterloo, Ontario: Wilfred Laurier University Press, 1984, pp. 169-184.

Siegman, Edward F. "St. Paul on the Redemptive Death of Christ." *Word and Mystery,* ed. by Leo J. O'Donovan. Glen Rock, NJ: Newman Press, 1968, pp. 87-108.

* Stanley, David Michael. *Christ's Resurrection in Pauline Soteriology. Rome: Pontifical Biblical Institute Press, 1961.*

_____ "Christ the Last Adam." *A Companion to Paul. Readings in Pauline Theology,* ed. by M. J. Taylor. New York: Alba House, 1975, pp. 13-22.

28
Christ's Saving Work in the New Testament

Best, E. *The Temptation and the Passion: The Markan Soteriology.* New York: Cambridge University Press, 1965.

Blackman, Edwin Cyril. "Reconciliation, Reconcile." *The Interpreter's Dictionary of the Bible,* ed. by G. A. Buttrick et al. Nashville, TN: Abingdon, 1962, vol. 4, pp. 16-17.

Boismard, M. E. "Jesus the Savior According to Saint John." *Word and Mystery,* ed. by Leo J. O'Donovan. Glen Rock, NJ: Newman Press, 1968, pp. 69-85.

Buchsel, Friedrich. "Katallasso." *Theological Dictionary of the New Testament,* ed. by G. Kittel, trans. by G. W. Bromiley. Grand Rapids, MI: Wm. B. Eerdmans, 1964, vol. 1, pp. 254-259.

_____ "Agorazo, exagorazo." *Theological Dictionary of the New Testament,* ed. by G. Kittel, trans. by G. W. Bromiley. Grand Rapids, MI: Wm. B. Eerdmans, 1964, vol. 1, pp. 124-128.

_____ "Lutron." *Theological Dictionary of the New Testament,* ed. by G. Kittel, trans. by G. W. Bromiley.

Grand Rapids, MI: Wm. B. Eerdmans, 1964, vol. 4, pp. 340-356.

Fitzmyer, Joseph A. "Pauline Soteriology." *The Jerome Biblical Commentary,* ed. by R. E. Brown & J. A. Fitzmyer. Englewood Cliffs, NJ: Prentice-Hall, Inc., 1968, vol. II, pp. 805-817.

Grelot, Pierre. "Christ's Duel with Death." *Dictionary of Biblical Theology,* ed. by X. Leon-Dufour, trans. by P.J. Cahill & E.M. Stewart. New York: The Seabury Press, 1973, pp. 117-119.

* Hengel, Martin. *The Atonement. The Origins of the Doctrine in the New Testament.* John Bowden, trans. Philadelphia: Fortress Press, 1981.

Hultgren, Arland J. *Christ and His Benefits. Christology and Redemption in the New Testament.* Philadelphia, PA: Fortress Press, 1987.

Link, Hans-George; Brown, Colin & Vorlander, Herwart. "Reconciliation, Restoration, Propitiation, Atonement." *The New International Dictionary of New Testament Theology,* Grand Rapids, MI: Zondervan, 1978, vol. 3, pp. 145-176.

Lyonnet, Stanislas. "Redemption." *Dictionary of Biblical Theology,* 2nd Ed., ed. by X. Leon-Dufour, trans. by P. J. Cahill & E. M. Stewart. New York: The Seabury Press, 1973, pp. 481-484.

Mitton, C. Leslie. "Atonement." *The Interpreter's Dictionary of the Bible,* ed. by G. A. Buttrick et al., Nashville, TN: Abingdon, 1962, vol. 1, pp. 309-313.

Mundle, Wilhelm; Brown, Colin & Schneider, Walter. "Redemption, Loose, Ransom, Deliverance, Release, Salvation, Savior." *The New International Dictionary of New Testament Theology,* ed. by C. Brown. Grand Rapids, MI: Zondervan, 1978, vol. 3, pp. 177-223.

O'Neill, J. C. "Did Jesus Teach that His Death Would Be Vicarious as Well as Typical?" *Suffering and Martyrdom in the New Testament,* ed. by W. Horbury & B. McNeill. Cambridge: Cambridge University Press, 1981, pp. 9-27.

Roy, Leon. "Reconciliation." *Dictionary of Biblical Theology,* ed. by X. Leon-Dufour, trans. by P.J. Cahill & E.M. Stewart. New York: The Seabury Press, 1973, pp. 479-480.

Siegmann, Edward F. "St. Paul on the Redemptive Death of Christ." *Word and Mystery,* ed. by Leo J. O'Donovan. Glen Rock, NJ: Newman Press, 1968, pp. 87-108.

Stanley, David M. "Christ as Savior in the Primitive Christian Preaching." *Word and Mystery,* ed. by Leo J. O'Donovan. Glen Rock, NJ: Newman Press, 1968, pp. 21-46.

_____ "Christ as Savior in the Synoptic Gospels." *Word and Mystery,* ed. by Leo J. O'Donovan. Glen Rock, NJ: Newman Press, 1968, pp. 47-67.

_____ *Christ's Resurrection in Pauline Soteriology.* Rome: Pontifical Biblical Institute Press, 1961.

* Taylor, Vincent. *The Atonement in New Testament Theology.* London: Macmillan & Co., 1940.

Vawter, Bruce. "Resurrection and Redemption." *Word and Mystery,* ed. by Leo J. O'Donovan. Glen Rock, NJ: Newman Press, 1968, pp. 231-244.

Williams, S. K. *Jesus' Death as a Saving Event. The Background and Origin of a Concept.* Missoula, MT: Scholars Press, 1975.

29
Christ's Death in
New Testament Theology

Abba, Raymond. "Expiation." *The Interpreter's Dictionary of the Bible,* ed. by G. A. Buttrick et al. Nashville, TN: Abingdon, 1962, vol. 2, pp. 200-201.

——————— "Propitiation." *The Interpreter's Dictionary of the Bible,* ed. by G. A. Buttrick et al. Nashville, TN: Abingdon, 1962, vol. 3, pp. 920-921.

Aquinas, Thomas *Summa Theologiae,* III, 46-47 and 50-52.

Benoit, Pierre. *The Passion and Resurrection of Jesus Christ.* B. Weatherhead, trans. New York: Herder and Herder, 1969.

Crowe, Jerome. "The Laos at the Cross: Luke's Crucifixion Scene." *The Language of the Cross,* ed. by A. Lacomara. Chicago: Franciscan Herald Press, 1977, pp. 75-101.

Hauret, Charles. "Sacrifice." *Dictionary of Biblical Theology,* 2nd. Ed., ed. by X. Leon-Dufour, trans., by P. J. Cahill & E. M. Stewart. New York: The Seabury Press, 1973, pp. 512-515.

Lacomara, Aelred. "The Death of Jesus as Revelation in John's Gospel." *The Language of the Cross,* ed. by A. Lacomara. Chicago: Franciscan Herald Press, 1977, pp. 103-127.

Lyonnet, Stanislas. "Expiation."*Dictionary of Biblical Theology,* 2nd. Ed., ed. by X. Leon-Dufour, trans., by P. J. Cahill & E. M. Stewart. New York: The Seabury Press, 1973, pp. 155-156.

McCarthy, Dennis J. "Blood." *The Interpreter's Dictionary of the Bible,* ed. by Keith Crim et al., Nashville, TN: Abingdon, 1976, Supp. Vol., pp. 114-117.

Moltmann, Jurgen. *The Crucified God. The Cross of Christ as the Foundation and Criticism of Christian Theology.* New York: Harper & Row, 1974.

* O'Collins, Gerald. *The Calvary Christ.* Philadelphia: The Westminster Press, 1977.

O'Neill, J. C. "Did Jesus Teach that His Death Would Be Vicarious as Well as Typical?" *Suffering and Martyrdom in the New Testament,* ed. by W. Horbury and B. McNeill. Cambridge: Cambridge University Press, 1981, pp. 9-27.

Rogers, Patrick. "The Desolation of Jesus in the Gospel of Mark." *The Language of the Cross,* ed. by A. Lacomara. Chicago: Franciscan Herald Press, 1977, pp. 55-74.

* Senior, Donald. "The Death of God's Son and the Beginning of the New Age (Matthew 27:51-54)." *The Language of the Cross,* ed. by A. Lacomara. Chicago: Franciscan Herald Press, 1977, pp. 29-51.

Thiele, Friedrich and Brown, Colin. "Sacrifice, First Fruits, Altar, Offering." *The New International Dictionary of New Testament Theology,* ed. by C. Brown. Grand Rapids, MI: Zondervan, 1978, vol. 3, pp. 415-438.

Weber, Hans-Ruedi. *The Cross. Tradition and Interpretation.* E. Jewett, trans. Grand Rapids, MI: Wm. B. Eerdmans, 1979.

* Williams, S.K. *Jesus' Death as a Saving Event. The Background and Origin of a Concept.* Missoula, MT: Scholars Press, 1975.

30
Christ's Resurrection in New Testament Theology

Alsup, John E. *The Post-Resurrection Appearance Stories in the Gospel Tradition. A History-of-Tradition Analysis.* London: SPCK, 1975.

Benoit, Pierre. *The Passion and Resurrection of Jesus Christ.* B. Weatherhead, trans. New York: Herder & Herder, 1969.

Bode, Edward Lynn. *The First Easter Morning. The Gospel Accounts of the Women's Visit to the Tomb of Jesus.* Rome: Biblical Institute Press, 1970.

* Brown, Raymond E. "The Problem of the Bodily Resurrection of Jesus." *The Virginal Conception and Bodily Resurrection of Jesus.* New York: Paulist Press, 1973, pp. 69-129.

Carlston, C. E. "Transfiguration and Resurrection." *Journal of Biblical Literature* 80 (1961), pp. 233-240.

Cavallin, H. C. C. *Life After Death. Paul's Argument for the Resurrection of the Dead in I Cor 15—An Inquiry into the Jewish Background.* Lund: Gleerup, 1974.

Coenen, Lothar and Brown, Colin. "Resurrection." *The New International Dictionary of New Testament*

Theology, ed. by C. Brown. Grand Rapids, MI: Zondervan, 1978, vol. 3, pp. 250-309.

Comblin, Joseph. *The Resurrection in the Plan of Salvation.* Sr. David Mary, trans. Notre Dame, IN: Fides Publishers. 1966.

Crossan, John Dominic. "Empty Tomb and Absent Lord (Mark 16:1-8)." *The Passion in Mark,* ed. by W. Kelber. Philadelphia: Fortress Press, 1976, pp. 135-152.

de Surgy, P., et al. *The Resurrection and Modern Biblical Thought.* C. U. Quinn, trans. New York: Corpus Books, 1970.

Derrett, J. Duncan M. *The Anastasis. The Resurrection of Jesus as an Historical Event.* Shipston-on-Stour, Warwickshire, England: P. Drinkwater, 1982.

* Durwell, F. X. *The Resurrection. A Biblical Study.* New York: Sheed and Ward, 1960.

Evans, C. F. *Resurrection and the New Testament.* Napierville, IL: Alec R. Allenson Inc., 1970.

* Fuller, Reginald H. *The Formation of the Resurrection Narratives.* New York: Macmillan Co., 1971.

Gaster, Theodore H. "Resurrection." *The Interpreter's Dictionary of the Bible,* ed. by G. A. Buttrick et al. Nashville, TN: Abingdon, 1962, vol. 4, pp. 39-43.

Grelot, Pierre. "The Resurrection of Jesus: Its Biblical and Jewish Background." *The Resurrection and Modern Biblical Thought,* ed. by P. de Surgy et al. New York: Corpus Books, 1970, pp. 1-29.

Jansen, John Frederick. *The Resurrection of Jesus Christ in New Testament Theology.* Philadelphia: The Westminster Press, 1980.

Kasemann, Ernst. *Jesus Means Freedom.* Philadelphia: Fortress Press, 1968.

Lampe, G.W.H. and MacKinnon, D.M. *The Resurrection. A Dialogue.* W. Purcell, ed. Philadelphia: The Westminster Press, 1967.

Layton, Bentley, ed. *The Gnostic Treatise on Resurrection from Nag Hammadi. Edited with Translation and Commentary.* Missoula, MT: Scholars Press, 1979.

Leon-Dufour, Xavier. *Resurrection and the Message of Easter.* R. N. Wilson, trans. New York: Holt, Rinehart and Winston, 1975.

_____ "The Appearances of the Risen Lord and Hermeneutics." *The Resurrection and Modern Biblical Thought,* ed. by P. de Surgy et al. New York: Corpus Books, 1970, pp. 107-128.

Loewe, W. P. "Appearances of the Risen Lord: Faith, Fact and Objectivity." *Horizons* 6 (1979), pp. 177-192.

Marxsen, Willi. *The Resurrection of Jesus of Nazareth.* Philadelphia: Fortress Press, 1970.

Minear, Paul S. *To Live and to Die. Christ's Resurrection and Christian Vocation.* New York: The Seabury Press, 1977.

Moule, C. F. D., ed. *The Significance of the Message of the Resurrection for Faith in Jesus Christ.* Napierville, IL: Alec R. Allenson Inc., 1968.

_____ "The Post-Resurrection Appearances in the Light of Festival Pilgrimages." *New Testament Studies* 4 (1957), pp. 58-61.

* O'Collins, Gerald. *What Are They Saying About the Resurrection?* New York: Paulist Press, 1978.

* _____ *The Easter Christ.* New Edition. London: Darton, Longman & Todd, 1980.

_____ *The Resurrection of Jesus Christ.* Valley Forge, PA: Judson Press, 1973.

Oepke, Albrecht. "anistemi." *Theological Dictionary of the New Testament,* ed. by G. Kittel, trans. by G. W. Bromiley. Grand Rapids, MI: Wm. B. Eerdmans, 1964, vol. 1, pp. 368-372.

_____ "egeiro." *Theological Dictionary of the New Testament,* ed. by G. Kittel, trans. by G. W. Bromiley. Grand Rapids, MI: Wm. B. Eerdmans, 1964, vol. 2, pp. 333-339.

* Perkins, Pheme. *Resurrection. New Testament Witness and Contemporary Reflection.* Garden City, NY: Doubleday & Co., 1984.

Perrin, Norman. *The Resurrection According to Matthew, Mark and Luke.* Philadelphia: Fortress Press, 1977.

Rademakers, Jean and Grelot, Pierre. "Resurrection." *Dictionary of Biblical Theology,* ed. by X. Leon-Dufour, trans. by P. J. Cahill & E. M. Stewart. New York: The Seabury Press, 1973, pp. 494-499.

Robinson, John A. T. "Resurrection in the NT." *The Interpreter's Dictionary of the Bible,* ed. by G. A. Buttrick et al. Nashville, TN: Abingdon, 1962, vol. 4, pp. 43-53.

Saunders, Ernest W. "Resurrection in the NT." *The Interpreter's Dictionary of the Bible,* ed. by Keith Crim et al., Nashville, TN: Abingdon, 1976, Supp. Vol., pp. 739-741.

Stanley, David Michael. *Christ's Resurrection in Pauline Soteriology.* Rome: Pontifical Biblical Institute Press, 1961.

Stein, R. H. "Is the Transfiguration (Mk 9:2-8) a Misplaced Resurrection Account? *Journal of Biblical Literature* 96 (1976), pp. 79-96.

Vawter, Bruce. "Resurrection and Redemption." *Word and Mystery,* ed. by Leo J. O'Donovan. Glen Rock, NJ: Newman Press, 1968, pp. 231-244.

Walker, W. D. "Post-Crucifixion Appearances and Christian Origins." *Journal of Biblical Literature* 88 (1969), pp. 157-165.

Ware, R. C. "The Resurrection of Jesus." *Heythrop Journal* 16 (1975) pp. 22-35; 174-194.

Wilckens, Ulrich. *Resurrection, Biblical Testimony to the Resurrection. An Historical Examination and Explanation.* Atlanta: John Knox Press, 1978.

31
New Testament Titles:
General Studies

* Hahn, Ferdinand. *The Titles of Jesus in Christology. Their History in Early Christianity.* New York: World Publishing Co., 1969.

Kramer, Werner. *Christ, Lord, Son of God.* B. Hardy, trans. Napierville, IL: Alec R. Allenson, Inc., 1966.

* Malina, Bruce J. and Neyrey, Jerome H. *Calling Jesus Names. The Social Value of Labels in Matthew.* Sonoma, CA: Polebridge Press, 1988.

* O'Grady, John F. *Jesus, Lord and Christ.* New York: Paulist Press, 1973.

Sabourin, Leopold. *The Names and Titles of Jesus. Themes of Biblical Theology.* New York: The Macmillan Co., 1967.

32
New Testament Titles: Christ / Messiah

Bonnard, Pierre-Emile and Grelot, Pierre. "Messiah." *Dictionary of Biblical Theology*, ed. by X. Leon-Dufour, trans. by P.J. Cahill & E.M. Stewart. New York: The Seabury Press, 1973, pp. 354-357.

Brownlee, William H. "Messianic Motifs of Qumran and the New Testament." *New Testament Studies* 3 (1956/57), pp. 12-30; 195-210.

de Jonge, Marinus. "The Use of the Word 'Anointed' in the Time of Jesus." *Novum Testamentum* 8 (1966), pp. 132-148.

Jenni, Ernst. "Messiah, Jewish." *The Interpreter's Dictionary of the Bible*, ed. by G.A. Buttrick et al. Nashville, TN: Abingdon, 1962, vol. 3, pp. 360-365.

Johnson, Sherman E. "Christ." *The Interpreter's Dictionary of the Bible*, ed. by G.A. Buttrick et al. Nashville, TN: Abingdon, 1962, vol. 1, pp. 563-571.

Juel, Donald. *Messianic Exegesis. Christological Interpretation of the Old Testament in Early Christianity.* Philadelphia, PA: Fortress Press, 1987.

Mowinckel, Sigmund. *He That Cometh. The Messiah Concept in the Old Testament and Later Judaism.* G.W. Anderson, trans. Nashville, TN: Abingdon 1954.

Rengstorf, Karl Heinrich. "Christos/Christ." *The New International Dictionary of New Testament Theology*, ed. by C. Brown. Grand Rapids, MI: Zondervan, 1976, vol. 2, pp. 334-343.

Ringgren, Helmer. *The Messiah in the Old Testament.* London: SCM Press, 1956.

Rivkin, Ellis. "Messiah, Jewish." *The Interpreter's Dictionary of the Bible*, ed. by Keith Crim et al., Nashville, TN: Abingdon, 1976, Supp. Vol., pp. 588-591.

33
New Testament Titles: Lord

Fitzmyer, Joseph A. "The Semitic Background of the New Testament Kyrios Title." *A Wandering Aramean. Aramaic Essays.* Missoula, MT: Scholars Press, 1979, pp. 115-142.

Foerster, Werner and Quell, Gottfried. "Kyrios." *Theological Dictionary of the New Testament*, ed. by G. Kittel, trans. by G.W. Bromiley. Grand Rapids, MI: Wm. B. Eerdmans, 1965, vol. 3, pp. 1039-1098.

Johnson, Sherman E. "Lord (Christ)." *The Interpreter's Dictionary of the Bible*, ed. by G.A. Buttrick et al. Nashville, TN: Abingdon, 1962, vol. 3, p. 151.

Ternant, Paul. "Lord." *Dictionary of Biblical Theology*, ed. by X. Leon-Dufour, trans. by P.J. Cahill & E.M. Stewart. New York: The Seabury Press, 1973, pp. 321-322.

34

New Testament Titles: Servant

Augrain, Charles and Lacan, Marc-Francois. "Servant of God." *Dictionary of Biblical Theology*, ed. by X. Leon-Dufour, trans. by P.J. Cahill & E.M. Stewart. New York: The Seabury Press, 1973, pp. 531-533.

* Manson, T.W. *The Servant-Messiah. A Study of the Public Ministry of Jesus.* New York: Cambridge University Press, 1953.

Michel, O. and Marshall, H. "pais Theou/Servant of God." *The New International Dictionary of New Testament Theology*, ed. by C. Brown. Grand Rapids, MI: Zondervan, 1978, vol. 3, pp. 607-613.

North, Christopher R. "Servant of the Lord." *The Interpreter's Dictionary of the Bible*, ed. by G.A. Buttrick et al. Nashville, TN: Abingdon, 1962, vol. 4, pp. 292-294.

Zimmerlin, Walter and Jeremias, Joachim. *The Servant of God.* Revised Edition. London: SCM Press, 1965.

35
New Testament Titles: Son of God

Anderson, Bernhard. "The Messiah as Son of God: Peter's Confession in Traditio-historical Perspective." *Christological Perspectives*, ed. by R.F. Berkey & S.A. Edwards. New York: Pilgrim Press, 1982, pp. 157-169.

* Brown, Raymond E. *Jesus God and Man. Modern Biblical Reflections.* Milwaukee: Bruce, 1967.

Haag, Herbert L. "'Son of God' in the Language and Thinking of the Old Testament." *Jesus, Son of God ?*, ed. by E. Schillebeeckx and J.-B. Metz. New York: The Seabury Press, 1982, pp. 31-36.

* Hengel, Martin. *The Son of God. The Origin of Christology and the History of Jewish-Hellenistic Religion.* Philadelphia: Fortress Press, 1976.

Johnson, Sherman E. "Son of God." *The Interpreter's Dictionary of the Bible*, ed. by G.A. Buttrick et al. Nashville, TN: Abingdon, 1962, vol. 4, pp. 408-413.

McDermott, J.M. "Jesus and the Son of God Title." *Gregorianum* 62 (1981), pp. 277-318.

Renard, Henri and Grelot, Pierre. "Son of God." *Dictionary of Biblical Theology*, ed. by X. Leon-Dufour, trans. by P.J. Cahill & E.M. Stewart. New York: The Seabury Press, 1973, pp. 561-563.

Van Iersel, Bas. "'Son of God' in the New Testament." *Jesus, Son of God?*, ed. by E. Schillebeeckx and J.-B. Metz. New York: The Seabury Press, 1982, pp. 37-48.

Wulfing von Martitz, P., et al. "Huios." *Theological Dictionary of the New Testament*, ed. by G. Friedrich, trans. by G. W. Bromiley. Grand Rapids, MI: Wm. B. Eerdmans, 1972, vol. 8, pp. 334-399.

36
New Testament Titles: Son of Man

Borsch, Frederick Houk. *The Son of Man in Myth and History*. Philadelphia: The Westminster Press, 1967.

Bowker, J. "The Son of Man." *Journal of Theological Studies* 28 (1977), pp. 19-48.

Casey, Maurice. *Son of Man. The Interpretation and Influence of Daniel* 7. London: SPCK, 1979.

Colpe, Carsten. "Ho Huios tou Anthropou." *Theological Dictionary of the New Testament*, ed. by G. Friedrich, trans. by G.W. Bromiley. Grand Rapids, MI: Wm. B. Eerdmans, 1972, vol. 8, pp. 400-477.

Delorme, Jean. "Son of Man." *Dictionary of Biblical Theology*, ed. by X. Leon-Dufour, trans. by P.J. Cahill & E.M. Stewart. New York: The Seabury Press, 1973, pp. 563-565.

Fitzmyer, Joseph A. "The New Testament Title 'Son of Man' Philologically Considered." *A Wandering Aramean. Aramaic Essays*. Missoula, MT: Scholars Press, 1979, pp. 143-160.

Fuller, Reginald H. "The Son of Man: A Reconsideration." *The Living Text*, ed. by D.E. Groh & R. Jewett. Lanham, MD: University Press of America, 1985, pp. 207-217.

* Higgins, A.J.B. *The Son of Man in the Teaching of Jesus.*
  New York: Cambridge University Press, 1980.

  _____ *Jesus and the Son of Man.* Philadelphia:
  Fortress Press, 1964.

Hooker, Morna D. *The Son of Man in Mark.* Montreal:
McGill University Press, 1967.

Johnson, Sherman E. "Son of Man." *The Interpreter's
Dictionary of the Bible*, ed. by G.A. Buttrick et al.
Nashville, TN: Abingdon, 1962, vol. 4, pp. 413-420.

Kraeling, Carl H. *Anthropos and Son of Man. A Study in
the Religious Syncretism of the Hellenistic Orient.*
New York: AMS Press Inc., 1966 reprint; orig. ed.
1927.

Leivestad, Ragnar. "Exit the Apocalyptic Son of Man."
New Testament Studies 18 (1972), pp. 243-267.

Lindars, Barnabas. *Jesus Son of Man: A Fresh Examination
of the Son of Man Sayings in the Gospels.* Grand
Rapids, MI: Wm. B. Eerdmans Publishing Co., 1983.

  _____ "Re-enter the Apocalyptic Son of Man." *New
  Testament Studies* 22 (1975), pp. 55-72.

Michel, O. and Marshall, I.H. "ho Huios tou anthropou/the
Son of Man." *The New International Dictionary of
New Testament Theology*, ed. by C. Brown. Grand
Rapids, MI: Zondervan, 1978, vol. 3, pp. 613-634.

Moloney, Francis J. *The Johannine Son of Man.* Rome:
Libreria Ateneo Salesiano, 1976.

Perrin, Norman. "Son of Man." *The Interpreter's Dictionary
of the Bible*, ed. by Keith Crim et al., Nashville, TN:
Abingdon, 1976, Supp. Vol., pp. 833-836.

Roth, Wolfgang. "Jesus as the Son of Man: The Scriptural
Identity of the Johannine Image." *The Living Text*,
ed. by D.E. Groh & R. Jewett. Lanham, MD:
University Press of America, 1985, pp. 11-26.

* Todt, H.E. *The Son of Man in the Synoptic Tradition.* London: SCM Press, 1965.

Vermes, Geza. "The Use of Bar Nash/Bar Nasha in Jewish Aramaic." *Post-Biblical Jewish Studies.* Leiden: E.J. Brill, 1975, pp. 147-165.

IV. Christ In Historical Dogmatic Theology

37
Dogmatic History and Controversy

Adam, Karl. *The Christ of Faith. The Christology of the Church.* New York: Pantheon Books, 1957.

Aldwinckle, Russell F. *More Than Man. A Study in Christology.* Grand Rapids, MI: William B. Eerdmans Publishing Co., 1976.

Chestnut, R.C. *Three Monophysite Christologies. Severus of Antioch, Philoxenus of Mabbug, and Jacob of Sarug.* New York: Oxford University Press, 1976.

Creasey, Maurice A. *Early Quaker Christology. With Special Reference to the Teaching and Significance of Isaac Pennington 1616-1679.* Manasquan, NJ: Catholic and Quaker Studies, 1956.

Deschner, John. *Wesley's Christology. An Interpretation.* Dallas, TX: Southern Methodist University Press, 1960.

Fabri, Enrique. "Docetism." *Sacramentum Mundi. An Encyclopedia of Theology,* ed. by K. Rahner et al. New York: Herder & Herder, 1968, vol. 2, pp. 94-95.

Frivold, Leif. *The Incarnation. A Study of the Doctrine of the Incarnation in the 5th and 6th Century Armenian Church.* Oslo: Universitetsforlaget, 1981.

* Grillmeier, Alois. *Christ in Christian Tradition. From the Apostolic Age to Chalcedon (451)*. 2nd Ed. Atlanta: John Knox Press, 1975.

_____ "Jesus Christ. III. Christology." *Sacramentum Mundi. An Encyclopedia of Theology*, ed. by K. Rahner et al. New York: Herder & Herder, 1969, vol. 3, p. 186-193.

_____ "Monophysitism." *Sacramentum Mundi. An Encyclopedia of Theology*, ed. by K. Rahner et al. New York: Herder & Herder, 1969, vol. 4, pp. 107-109.

Lohse, Bernhard. *A Short History of Christian Doctrine*. F. Ernest Stoeffler, trans. Philadelphia: Fortress Press, 1966, pp. 37-99.

* Lonergan, Bernard J.F. *The Way to Nicaea. The Dialectical Development of Trinitatian Theology*. Philadelphia: The Westminster Press, 1976.

MacKinnon, D.M. "'Substance' in Christology—A Cross-Bench View." *Christ Faith and History*, ed. by S.W. Sykes & J.P. Clayton. New York: Cambridge University Press, 1972, pp. 279-300.

Marcus, Wolfgang. "Arianism." *Sacramentum Mundi. An Encyclopedia of Theology*, ed. by K. Rahner et al. New York: Herder & Herder, 1968, vol. 1, pp. 95-97.

* Murphy, F.X. "Christological Controversy, Early." *New Catholic Encyclopedia*. New York: McGraw-Hill, 1967, vol. 3, pp. 660-662.

Niebuhr, Richard R. *Schleiermacher on Christ and Religion. A New Introduction*. New York: Charles Scribner's Sons, 1964.

Papadakis, Aristedes. *Crisis in Byzantium. The Filioque Controversy in the Patriarchate of Gregory II of Cyprus (1283-1289)*. New York: Fordham University Press, 1983.

Pelikan, Jaroslav. *The Christian Tradition/I. The Emergence of the Catholic Tradition (100-600).* Chicago: University of Chicago Press, 1971, esp. pp. 172-277.

Rahner, Karl. "Jesus Christ. IV. History of Dogma and Theology." *Sacramentum Mundi. An Encyclopedia of Theology,* ed. by K. Rahner et al. New York: Herder & Herder, 1969, vol. 3, pp. 192-209.

Schmaus, Michael. *God and His Christ.* Kansas City, KS: Sheed and Ward, 1971.

Siggins, Jan D. Kingston. *Martin Luther's Doctrine of Christ.* New Haven: Yale University Press, 1970.

Sykes, S.W. and Clayton, J.P., eds. *Christ Faith and History. Cambridge Studies in Christology.* New York: Cambridge University Press, 1972.

Walsh, J.J. "Christology." *New Catholic Encyclopedia.* New York: McGraw-Hill, 1967, vol. 3, pp. 662-663.

Wiles, M.F. "Does Christology Rest on a Mistake?" *Christ Faith and History,* ed. by S.W. Sykes & J.P. Clayton, New York: Cambridge University Press, 1972, pp. 3-12.

38
Patristic Christology

Abramowski, Luise and Goodman, Alan E. *A Nestorian Collection of Christological Texts. 2 vols. Syriac Text, Translation.* Cambridge: Cambridge University Press, 1972.

Athanasius, St. *On the Incarnation.* Translation of the Treatise "De Incarnatione Verbi Dei." Introduction by C.S. Lewis. Crestwood, NY: St. Vladimir's Seminary Press, 1982 reprint; first ed. 1944.

Beskow, Per. *Rex Gloriae. The Kingship of Christ in the Early Church.* Stockholm: Almquist & Wiksell, 1962.

Bettenson, Henry, ed. *The Later Christian Fathers. A Selection from the Writings of the Fathers from St. Cyril of Jerusalem to St. Leo the Great.* New York: Oxford University Press, 1970.

Carmody, James M. and Clarke, Thomas E., eds. *Word and Redeemer. Christology in the Fathers.* Glen Rock, NJ: Paulist Press, 1966.

Evans, David Beecher. *Leontius of Byzantium. An Origenist Christology.* Washington: Dumbarton Oaks center for Byzantine Studies, 1970.

* Hardy, Edward Roche, with Richardson, C.C., eds. *Christology of the Later Fathers*. Philadelphia: Westminster Press, 1954.

Heron, Alasdair. "'Logos, Image, Son.' Some Models and Paradigms in Early Christianity." *Creation, Christ and Culture*, ed. by R.W.A. McKinney. Edinburgh: T. & T. Clark Ltd., 1976, pp. 43-62.

Little, V.A. Spence. *The Christology of the Apologists*. New York: Charles Scribner's Sons, 1935.

Norris, R.A. *Manhood and Christ. A Study in the Christology of Theodore of Mopsuestia*. London: Oxford University Press, 1963.

Norris, Richard A., Jr., translator/ editor. *The Christological Controversy*. Philadelphia: Fortress Press, 1980.

Pelikan, Jaroslav. *The Light of the World. A Basic Image in Early Christian Thought*. New York: Harper & Brothers, 1962.

Pollack, Andrew J. *The Blood of Christ in Greek Literature Till the Year 444 A.D.* Carthagena, OH: The Messenger Press, 1956.

Pollard, T.E. *Johannine Christology and the Early Church*. Cambridge: Cambridge University Press, 1970.

Raven, Charles E. *Apollinarianism. An Essay on the Christology of the Early Church*. New York: AMS Press, Inc., 1978 reprint; first ed. 1923.

* Smulders, P. *The Fathers on Christology. The Development of Christological Dogma from the Bible to the Great Councils*. L. Roy, trans. DePere, WI: St. Norbert Abbey Press, 1968.

Trakatellis, Demetrius Christ. *The Pre-Existence of Christ in the Writings of Justin Martyr*. Missoula, MT: Scholars Press, 1976.

Turner, H.E.W. *The Patristic Doctrine of Redemption. A Study of the Development of Doctrine During the First Five Centuries.* London: A.R. Mowbray & Co., 1952.

Van Bavel, Tarsicius. "Chalcedon: Then and Now." *Jesus, Son of God?* ed. by E. Schillebeeckx and J.-B. Metz. New York: The Seabury Press, 1982, pp. 55-62.

Wainwright, Geoffrey. "'Son of God' in Liturgical Doxologies." *Jesus, Son of God?* ed. by E. Schillebeeckx and J.-B. Metz. New York: The Seabury Press, 1982, pp. 49-54.

Wingren, Gustaf. *Man and the Incarnation. A Study in the Biblical Theology of Irenaeus.* R. MacKenzie, trans., Philadelphia: Muhlenberg Press, 1959.

Young, Frances M. *The Use of Sacrificial Ideas in Greek Christian Writers from the New Testament to John Chrysostom.* Philadelphia: The Philadelphia Patristic Foundation, 1979.

39
Christology in Eastern Tradition

Bria, Ion. *Jesus Christ—The Life of the World. An Orthodox Contribution to the Vancouver Theme.* Geneva: The World Council of Churches, 1982.

Gorodetzky, Nadejda. *The Humiliated Christ in Modern Russian Thought.* New York: AMS Press, Inc., 1973 reprint; first ed. 1938.

Kesich, Veselin. *The First Day of Creation. The Resurrection and Christian Faith.* Crestwood, NY: St. Vladimir's Seminary Press, 1982.

Makrakis, Apostolos. *The Human Nature of Christ. Growth and Perfection.* D. Cummings, trans. Chicago: The Orthodox Christian Education Society, 1965.

* Meyendorff, John. *Christ in Eastern Christian Thought.* Washington: Corpus Books, 1969.

40
Incarnation

Adam, Karl. *Christ Our Brother.* J. McCann, trans. New York: The Macmillan Company, 1931.

——————. *The Son of God.* P. Hereford, trans. New York: Sheed & Ward, 1934.

Aldwinckle, Russell F. *More Than Man. A Study in Christology.* Grand Rapids, MI: William B. Eerdmans Publishing Co., 1976.

Aquinas, Thomas. *Summa Theologiae*, I, 34; III, 1-59.

* Baillie, D.M. *God Was In Christ. An Essay on Incarnation and Atonement.* New York: Charles Scribner's Sons, 1948.

Barth, Karl. *The Humanity of God.* Richmond: John Knox Press, 1970.

Blackman, Edwin Cyril. "Incarnation." *The Interpreter's Dictionary of the Bible*, ed. by G.A. Buttrick et al. Nashville, TN: Abingdon, 1962, vol. 2, pp. 691-697.

Bushnell, Horace. *God in Christ.* New York: AMS Press, Inc., 1972 reprint; first ed. 1849.

Dunn, J.D.G. *Christology in the Making. A New Testament Inquiry into the Origins of the Doctrine of the*

Incarnation. Philadelphia: The Westminster Press, 1980.

Forsyth, P.T. *The Person and Place of Jesus Christ*. Grand Rapids, MI: Wm. B. Eerdmans Publishing Co., n.d. reprint; original ed. 1909.

Galot, Jean. *Who is Christ? A Theology of Incarnation*. Chicago: Franciscan Herald Press, 1981.

——————— *The Person of Christ. A Theological Insight*. Chicago: Franciscan Herald Press, 1984.

Harvey, A.E., ed. *God Incarnate. Story and Belief*. London: SPCK, 1981.

Heron, A. "Doing Without the Incarnation?" *Scottish Journal of Theology* 31 (1978), pp. 51-71.

Lane, Dermot. "The Incarnation of God in Jesus." *Irish Theological Quarterly* 46 (1979), pp. 158-169.

MacKinnon, D.R. "The Relation of the Doctrines of the Incarnation and the Trinity." *Creation, Christ and Culture*, ed. by R.W.A. McKinney. Edinburgh: T. & T. Clarke Ltd., 1976, pp. 92-107.

Mascall, E.L. *Christ, The Christian and the Church. A Study of the Incarnation and its Consequences*. London: Longfmans, Green and Co., 1946.

Morris, Thomas V. *The Logic of God Incarnate*. Ithaca, NY: Cornell University Press, 1986.

Moule, C.F.D. "The Manhood of Jesus in the New Testament." *Christ Faith and History*, ed. by S.W. Sykes and J.P. Clayton. New York: Cambridge University Press, 1972, pp. 95-110.

Rahner, Karl. "On the Theology of the Incarnation." *Theological Investigations*, IV, trans. by K. Smyth. New York: Crossroad, 1982 reprint; first ET 1966, pp. 105-120.

_____. "The Quest for Approaches Leading to an Understanding of the Mystery of the God-Man Jesus." *Theological Investigations*, XIII, trans. by D. Bourke. New York: Crossroad, 1983 reprint; first ET 1975, pp. 195-200.

* _____ "Incarnation." *Sacramentum Mundi. An Encyclopedia of Theology*, ed. by K. Rahner et al. New York: Herder & Herder, 1968, vol, 3, pp. 110-118.

Robinson, John A.T. "Need Jesus Have Been Perfect? *Christ Faith and History*, ed. by S.W. Sykes and J.P. Clayton. New York: Cambridge University Press, 1972, pp. 39-52.

Stead, George Christopher. *Divine Substance*. Oxford: Clarendon Press, 1977.

Sykes, S.W. "The Theology of the Humanity of Christ." *Christ Faith and History*, ed. by S.W. Sykes & J.P. Clayton. New York: Cambridge. University Press, 1972, pp. 53-72.

Torrance, T.F. *The Mediation of Christ*. Grand Rapids, MI: Wm. B. Eerdmans Publishing Co., 1983.

_____ *Space, Time and Incarnation*. New York: Oxford University Press, 1969.

Wingren, G. Man and the Incarnation. A Study of the Biblical Theology of Irenaeus. R. MacKenzie, trans. Philadelphia: Muhlenberg Press, 1959.

Zizioulas, J.D. "Human Capacity and Human Incapacity." *Scottish Journal of Theology* 28 (1975), pp. 402-447.

41
Christ's Humanity

Aquinas, Thomas. *Summa Theologiae*, III, 5-6, 17-19, 40-41.

Brinkman, Bruno. "The Humanity of Christ I. Christ and Sexuality." *The Way* 15 (1975), pp. 209-224.

Johnson, Harry. *The Humanity of the Saviour. A Biblical and Historical Study of the Human Nature of Christ in Relation to Original Sin.* London: The Epworth Press, 1962.

Maritain, Jacques. *On the Grace and Humanity of Jesus.* J.W. Evans, trans. New York: Herder & Herder, 1969.

* North, Robert. *In Search of the Human Jesus.* New York: Corpus Books, 1970.

Rahner, Karl. "The Eternal Significance of the Humanity of Jesus for our Relationship with God." *Theological Investigations*, III, trans. by K.-H. Kruger. New York: Crossroad, 1982 reprint; first ET 1967, pp. 35-46.

42
Christ's Human Knowledge And Consciousness

Aquinas, Thomas. *Summa Theologiae*, III, 9-13.

Ashton, J. "The Consciousness of Christ." *The Way* 10 (1970), pp. 59-71, 147-157, 250-259.

* Brown, Raymond E. "How Much Did Jesus Know?" *Jesus. God and Man*. Milwaukee: Bruce Publishing Co., 1967, pp. 39-102.

Guillet, Jacques. *The Consciousness of Jesus*. E. Bonin, trans. New York: Newman Press, 1972.

Gutwenger, Engelbert. "The Problem of Christ's Knowledge." *Who is Jesus of Nazareth?* ed. by E. Schillebeeckx et al. New York: Paulist Press, 1965, pp. 91-105.

Lonergan, Bernard J.F. *De Constitutione Christi Ontologica et Psychologica*. 4th Edition. Rome: Gregorian University Press, 1964.

Murray, J.C. *The Infused Knowledge of Christ in the Theology of the 12th and 13th Centuries*. Rome: Pontificium Atneneum Angelicum, 1963.

Rahner, Karl. "Dogmatic Reflections on the Knowledge and Self-Consciousness of Christ." *Theological Investigations*, V., trans. by K.-H. Kruger. New York: Crossroad, 1983 reprint; first ET 1966; pp. 193-215.

Thompson, William M. *Christ and Consciousness. Exploring Christ's Contribution to Human Consciousness.* New York: Paulist Press, 1977.

43
Soteriology: General Questions

Berkouwer, G.C. *The Work of Christ.* Grand Rapids, MI: Wm. B. Eerdmans Publishing Co., 1965.

* Edwards, Denis. *What Are They Saying About Salvation?* New York: Paulist Press, 1986.

Farmer, H.H. *The Word of Reconciliation.* Nashville, TN: Abingdon, 1966.

* Guzie, Tad. *What a Modern Catholic Believes About Salvation.* Chicago: The Thomas More Press, 1975.

Kloppenburg, Bonaventure. *Christian Salvation and Human Temporal Progress.* Paul Burns, trans. Chicago: Franciscan Herald Press, 1979.

Lochman, Jan Milic. *Reconciliation and Liberation. Challenging a One-Dimensional View of Salvation.* David Lewis, trans. Philadelphia: Fortress Press, 1980.

Pfurtner, Stephen. *Luther and Aquinas on Salvation.* E. Quinn, trans. New York: Sheed and Ward, 1964.

* Taylor, Vincent. *Forgiveness and Reconciliation.* London: Macmillan & Co., 1960.

44
Soteriology: Atonement

* Aulen, Gustaf. *Christus Victor: An Historical Study of the Three Main Types of the Idea of the Atonement.* New York: Macmillan, 1969.

Dahl, Nils Alstrup. "The Atonement—An Adequate Reward for the Akedah." *The Crucified Messiah and Other Essays.* Minneapolis: Augsburg Publishing House, 1974, pp., 146-160.

De Rosa, Peter. *God Our Savior. A Study of the Atonement.* Milwaukee: Bruce Publishing Co., 1967.

Dillistone, Frederick W. *The Christian Understanding of the Atonement.* Philadelphia: The Westminster Press, 1968; London: SCM Press, 1984 reprint.

Milgrom, J. "Atonement in the OT." *The Interpreter's Dictionary of the Bible,* ed. by Keith Crim et al. Nashville, TN: Abingdon, 1976, Supp. Vol., pp. 78-82.

Nele, Herbert. *The Doctrine of the Atonement in the Theology of Wolfhart Pannenberg.* Berlin/New York: Walter de Gruyter, 1979.

Paul, Robert S. *The Atonement and the Sacraments. The Relation of the Sacraments of Baptism and the Lord's Supper.* London: Hodder & Stoughton, 1961.

Sheets, John R., ed. *The Theology of the Atonement. Readings in Soteriology.* Englewood Cliffs, NJ: Prentice-Hall, Inc., 1967.

Tull, James E. *The Atoning Gospel.* Macon, GA: Mercer University Press, 1982.

Wolf, William J. *No Cross, No Crown. A Study of the Atonement.* New York: The Seabury Press, 1967.

45
Soteriology: Christ's Sacrifice

Agnew, Barbara. "The Meaning of Jesus' Sacrifice." *Does Jesus Make a Difference?* ed. by T.M. McFadden. New York: The Seabury Press, 1974, pp. 143-163.

Barth, Markus. *Was Christ's Death a Sacrifice?* London: Oliver & Boyd, Ltd., 1961.

* Daly, R.J. *The Origins of the Christian Doctrine of Sacrifice.* Philadelphia: Fortress Press, 1978.

Hefner, P. "The Cultural Significance of Jesus' Death as Sacrifice." *Journal of Religion* 60 (1980), pp. 411-439.

Kendall, E.L. *A Living Sacrifice. A Study of Reparation.* London: SCM Press, 1960.

Moule, C.F.D. *The Sacrifice of Christ.* Philadelphia: Fortress Press, 1964.

* Young, Frances M. *Sacrifice and the Death of Christ.* Philadelphia: The Westminster Press, 1975.

_____ *The Use of Sacrificial Ideas in Greek Christian Writers from the New Testament to John Chrysostom.* Philadelphia: The Philadelphia Patristic Foundation, 1979.

46
Soteriology: Redemption

Aquinas, Thomas. *Summa Theologiae*, III, 48-49.

* De La Trinite, Philippe. *What is Redemption?* A. Armstrong, trans. New York: Hawthorn Books, 1961.

Richard, Louis. *The Mystery of the Redemption*. Baltimore: Helicon Press, 1965.

Robinson, H. Wheeler. *Redemption and Revelation in the Actuality of History*. London: Nisbet & Co. Ltd., 1942.

* Van Caster, Marcel. *The Redemption. A Personalist View*. Glen Rock, NJ: Paulist Press, 1965.

Willems, Boniface A. *The Reality of Redemption*. New York: Herder and Herder, 1970.

47
Theologia Crucis

Faricy, Robert. "Teilhard de Chardin's Theology of the Cross." *The Cross Today*, G. O'Collins et al. New York: Paulist Press, 1977, pp. 12-29.

Gorodetzky, Nadejda. *The Humiliated Christ in Modern Russian Thought*. New York: AMS Press, Inc., 1973 reprint; first ed. 1938.

Kasemann, Ernst. "The Saving Significance of the Death of Jesus in Paul." *Perspectives on Paul*, trans. by M. Kohl. Philadelphia: Fortress Press, 1971, pp. 32-59.

Kitamori, Kazo. *Theology of the Pain of God*. Richmond: John Knox Press, 1965.

* Lacomara, Aelred, ed. *The Language of the Cross*. Chicago: Franciscan Herald Press, 1977.

Loewe, William P. "Encountering the Crucified God: The Soteriology of Sebastian Moore." *Horizons* 9 (1982), pp. 216-236.

McGrath, Alister E. *Luther's Theology of the Cross. Martin Luther's Theological Breakthrough*. New York: Basil Blackwell, Inc., 1985.

O'Collins, Gerald, et al. *The Cross Today. An Evaluation of Current Theological Reflections on the Cross of Christ*. New York: Paulist Press, 1977.

Prenter, Regin. *Luther's Theology of the Cross*. Philadelphia: Fortress Press, 1971.

Rahner, Karl. "Following the Crucified." *Theological Investigations*, XVIII, trans. by E. Quinn. New York: Crossroad, 1983, pp. 157-170.

Ramlot, Marie-Leon. "Suffering." *Dictionary of Biblical Theology*, 2nd Ed., ed. by X. Leon-Dufour, trans. by P.J. Cahill & E.M. Stewart. New York: The Seabury Press, 1973, pp. 586-590.

Von Loewenich, W. *Luther's Theology of the Cross*. H.J.A. Bowman, trans. Minneapolis: Augsburg Publishing House, 1976.

Weeden, Theodore J. "The Cross as Power in Weakness (Mark 15:20b-41)." *The Passion in Mark*, ed. by W.H. Kelber. Philadelphia: Fortress Press, 1976, pp. 115-134.

48
Resurrection Theology

Aquinas, Thomas. *Summa Theologiae*, III, 53-56.

* Galvin, John. "The Resurrection of Jesus in Contemporary Catholic Systematics." *Heythrop Journal* 20 (1979), pp. 123-145.

Kunneth, Walter. *The Theology of the Resurrection.* J.W. Leitch, trans. St. Louis: Concordia Publishing House, 1965.

Loewe, W.P. "Appearances of the Risen Lord: Faith, Fact and Objectivity." *Horizons* 6 (1979), pp. 177-192.

Niebuhr, Richard R. *Resurrection and Historical Reason. A Study of Theological Method.* New York: Charles Scribner's Sons, 1957.

O'Collins, Gerald. "Jesus in Current Theology. III. Christ's Resurrection and our Imagination." *The Way* 17 (1977), pp. 135-144.

_____ "Karl Barth on Christ's Resurrection." *Scottish Journal of Theology*, 26 (1973), pp. 85-99.

* _____ *What Are They Saying About the Resurrection?* New York: Paulist Press, 1978.

Rahner, Karl. "Dogmatic Questions on Easter." *Theological Investigations,* IV, trans. by K. Smyth. New York: Crossroad, 1982 reprint; first ET 1966, pp. 121-133.

_____, Schmitt, J., and Bulst, W. "Resurrection of Christ." *Sacramentum Mundi. An Encyclopedia of Theology*, ed. by K. Rahner et al. New York: Herder & Herder, 1970, vol. 5, pp. 323-333.

Stendahl, K., ed. *Immortality and Resurrection*. New York: Macmillan, 1971.

Torrance, T.F. *Space, Time and Resurrection*. Grand Rapids, MI: Wm. B. Eerdmans Publishing Co., 1977.

49
Christ-Centered Spirituality

De Margerie, Bertrand. *Christ for the World—The Heart of the Lamb. A Treatise on Christology.* M. Carroll, trans. Chicago: Franciscan Herald Press, 1973.

Faricy, Robert. "Teilhard de Chardin's Spirituality of the Cross." *Horizons* 3 (1976), pp. 1-15.

Meilach, Michael D. *From Order to Omega.* Chicago: Franciscan Herald Press, 1967.

Moore, Sebastian. *Let this Mind Be In You. The Quest for Identity Through Oedipus to Christ.* Minneapolis: Winston Press, 1985.

—————— *No Exit.* Glen Rock, NJ: Newman Press, 1968.

Petrovits, Joseph Julius Charles. *Theology of the Cultus of the Sacred Heart. A Moral, Dogmatic and Historical Study.* Washington: Catholic University of America, 1917.

Rahner, Karl. "'Behold This Heart.' Preliminaries to a Theology of Devotion to the Sacred Heart." *Theological Investigations*, III, trans. by K.-H. Kruger. New York: Crossroad, 1982 reprint; first ET 1967, pp. 321-330.

_____ "Some Theses for a Theology of Devotion to the Sacred Heart." *Theological Investigations*, III, trans. by K.-H. Kruger. New York: Crossroad, 1982 reprint; first ET 1967, pp. 331-352.

Thompson, William M. "The Christic Universe of Pierre de Berulle and the French School." *American Benedictine Review*, 29 (1978), pp. 320-347.

V. Contemporary Approaches And Issues In Christology

50
Contemporary Christologies: General

Cobb, John. *Christ in a Pluralistic Age.* Philadelphia: The Westminster Press, 1975.

Congar, Yves. *Jesus Christ.* L. O'Neill, trans. New York: Herder and Herder, 1966.

Gray, Donald P. "The Incarnation. God's Giving and Man's Receiving." *Horizons* 1 (1974), pp. 1-13.

Hall, Thor. *The Evolution of Christology.* Nashville, TN: Abingdon, 1982.

* Hellwig, Monika. *Jesus. The Compassion of God. New Perspectives on the Tradition of Christianity.* Wilmington, DE: Michael Glazier, 1983.

Hodgson, Peter C. *Jesus—Word and Presence. An Essay in Christology.* Philadelphia: Fortress Press, 1971.

Kasper, Walter. *Jesus the Christ.* V. Green, trans. New York: Paulist Press, 1976.

Ketcham, Charles B. *A Theology of Encounter. The Ontological Ground for a New Christology.* University Park, PA: The Pennsylvania State University, 1978.

* Mackey, James. *Jesus. The Man and the Myth.* New York: Paulist Press, 1979.

Macquarrie, John. "Existentialist Christology." *Christological Perspectives*, ed. by R.F. Berkey & S. A. Edwards. New York: Pilgrim Press, 1982, pp. 228-237.

Nele, Herbert. *The Doctrine of the Atonement in the Theology of Wolfhart Pannenberg.* Berlin/New York: Walter de Gruyter, 1979.

O'Collins, Gerald. "Jesus in Current Theology. II. Salvation and Commitment." *The Way* 17 (1977), pp. 51-64.

Pannenberg, Wolfhart. *Jesus—God and Man.* Philadelphia: The Westminster Press, 1968.

Ritschl, Dietrich. *Memory and Hope. An Inquiry Concerning the Presence of Christ.* New York: Macmillan, 1967.

Robinson, John A.T. *The Human Face of God.* Philadelphia: The Westminster Press, 1973.

* Schillebeeckx, Edward. *Christ. The Experience of Jesus as Lord.* New York: Crossroad, 1981.

* _____ *Jesus. An Experiment in Christology.* New York: Crossroad, 1979.

_____ *Interim Report on the Books Jesus & Christ.* J. Bowden, trans. New York: Crossroad, 1981.

_____ and Metz, J.-B., eds. *Jesus, Son of God ?* New York: The Seabury Press, 1982.

Schoonenberg, Piet. *The Christ. A Study of the God-Man Relationship in the Whole of Creation and in Jesus Christ.* New York: The Seabury Press, 1971.

Sloyan, Gerard S. "Some Problems in Modern Christology." *A World More Human, a Church More Christian*, ed. by G. Devine. New York: Alba House, 1973, pp. 27-51.

Soelle, Dorothee. *Christ the Representative.* Philadelphia: Fortress Press, 1967.

Tavard, George H. *Images of Christ. An Enquiry into Christology.* Lanham, MD: University Press of America, 1982.

Thompson, William M. *Jesus, Lord and Savior. A Theopatic Christology and Soteriology.* New York: Paulist Press, 1980.

Van Beeck, Franz Jozef. *Christ Proclaimed. Christology as Rhetoric.* New York: Paulist Press, 1979.

51
Contemporary Christologies: Karl Rahner

Rahner, Karl. "Christology Today?" *Theological Investigations*, XVII, trans. by M. Kohl. New York: Crossroad, 1981, pp. 24-38.

——————— "Christology Within an Evolutionary View of the World." *Theological Investigations*, V, trans. by K.-H. Kruger. New York: Crossroad, 1983 reprint; first ET 1966, pp. 157-192.

——————— "Christology in the Setting of Modern Man's Understanding of Himself and His World." *Theological Investigations*, XI, trans. by D. Bourke. New York: Crossroad, 1982 reprint; first ET 1974, pp. 215-229.

* ——————— "Current Problems in Christology." *Theological Investigations*, I, trans. by C. Ernst. New York: Crossroad, 1982 reprint; first ET 1961, pp. 149-200.

——————— "Dogmatic Reflections on the Knowledge and Self-Consciousness of Christ." *Theological Investigations*, V, trans. by K.-H. Kruger. New York: Crossroad, 1983 reprint; first ET 1966, pp. 193-215.

_____ "Following the Crucified." *Theological Investigations*, XVIII, trans. by E. Quinn. New York: Crossroad, 1983, pp. 157-170.

_____ "Human Aspects of the Birth of Christ." *Theological Investigations*, XIII, trans. by D. Bourke. New York: Crossroad, 1983 reprint; first ET 1975, pp. 189-194.

_____ "Incarnation." *Sacramentum Mundi. An Encyclopedia of Theology*, ed. by K. Rahner et al. New York: Herder & Herder, 1968, vol. 3, pp. 110-118.

_____ "Jesus Christ in the Non-Christian Religions." *Theological Investigations*, XVII, trans. by M. Kohl. New York: Crossroad, 1981, pp. 39-50.

_____ "One Mediator and Many Mediations." *Theological Investigations*, IX, trans. by G. Harrison. New York: Herder & Herder, 1972, p. 169-184.

_____ "Oneness and Threefoldness of God in Discussion with Islam." *Theological Investigations*, XVIII, trans. by E. Quinn. New York: Crossroad, 1983, pp. 105-121.

_____ "On the Theology of the Incarnation." *Theological Investigations*, IV, trans. by K. Smyth. New York: Crossroad, 1982 reprint; first ET 1966, pp. 105-120.

_____ "Remarks on the Importance of the History of Jesus for Catholic Dogmatics." *Theological Investigations*, XIII, trans. by D. Bourke. New York: Crossroad, 1983 reprint; first ET 1975, pp. 201-212.

_____ "The Death of Jesus and the Closure of Revelation." *Theological Investigations,* XVIII, trans. by E. Quinn. New York: Crossroad, 1983, pp. 132-142.

_____ "The One Christ and the Universality of Salvation." *Theological Investigations*, XVI, trans. by

D. Morland. New York: Crossroad, 1983 reprint; first ET 1979, pp. 199-224.

* _____ "The Position of Christology in the Church Between Exegesis and Dogmatics." *Theological Investigations*, XI, trans. by D. Bourke. New York: Crossroad, 1982 reprint; first ET 1974, pp. 185-214.

_____ "The Quest for Approaches Leading to an Understanding of the Mystery of the God-Man Jesus." *Theological Investigations*, XIII, trans. by D. Bourke. New York: Crossroad, 1983 reprint; first ET 1975, pp. 195-200.

* _____ "The Two Basic Types of Christology." *Theological Investigations*, XIII, trans. by D. Bourke. New York: Crossroad, 1983 reprint; first ET 1975, pp. 213-223.

_____ and Thuesing, William. *A New Christology.* New York: The Seabury Press, 1980.

Wong, Joseph H.P. *Logos-Symbol in the Christology of Karl Rahner.* Foreword by Karl Rahner. Rome: Libreria Ateneo Salesiano, 1984.

52
Contemporary Christologies:
Liberation Theologians

Boff, Leonardo. *Jesus Christ Liberator. A Critical Christology for Our Time.* Maryknoll, NY: Orbis Books, 1978.

_____ *The Lord's Prayer. The Prayer of Integral Liberation.* Maryknoll, NY: Orbis Books, 1983.

Bussmann, Claus. *Who Do You Say? Jesus Christ in Latin American Theology.* Maryknoll, NY: Orbis Books, 1985.

Cleage, Albert. *The Black Messiah.* New York: Sheed & Ward, 1968.

* Cone, James H. *A Black Theology of Liberation.* Philadelphia: Lippincott, 1970.

Echegary, Hugo. *The Practice of Jesus.* M.J. O'Connell, trans. Maryknoll, NY: Orbis Books, 1984.

Kloppenburg, Bonaventure. *Christian Salvation and Human Temporal Progress.* Paul Burns, trans. Chicago: Franciscan Herald Press, 1979.

Miguez-Bonino, Jose, ed. *Faces of Christ: Latin American Christologies.* R.R. Barr, trans. Maryknoll, NY: Orbis Books, 1984.

Segundo, Juan Luis. *The Historical Jesus of the Synoptics.* Maryknoll, NY: Orbis Books, 1985.

——————— *The Humanist Christology of Paul.* J. Drury, trans. Maryknoll, NY: Orbis Books, 1986.

Sobrino, Jon. "A Crucified People's Faith in the Son of God." *Jesus, Son of God* ? ed. by E. Schillebeeckx and J.-B. Metz. New York: The Seabury Press, 1982, pp. 23-28.

* ——————— *Christology at the Crossroads.* Maryknoll, NY: Orbis Books, 1978.

53
Contemporary Christologies: Neo-Orthodoxy

* Barth, Karl. *Church Dogmatics*, IV/1, IV/2, IV/3-i, IV/3-ii. G. W. Bromiley, trans. Edinburgh: T. & T. Clark, 1956, 1958, 1961, 1962.

_____ *The Humanity of God.* Richmond: John Knox Press, 1970.

Berkouwer, G.C. *The Person of Christ.* Grand Rapids, MI: Wm. B. Eerdmans Publishing Co., 1954.

_____ *The Work of Christ.* Grand Rapids, MI: Wm. B. Eerdmans Publishing Co., 1965.

Bloesch, Donald G. *Jesus is Victor. Karl Barth's Doctrine of Salvation.* Nashville, TN: Abingdon, 1976.

Bonhoeffer, Dietrich. *Christ the Center.* New York: Harper & Row, 1960.

Brunner, Emil. *The Christian Doctrine of Creation and Redemption. Dogmatics II.* Olive Wyon, trans. Philadelphia: The Westminster Press, 1952.

_____ *The Mediator. A Study of the Central Doctrine of the Christian Faith.* Philadelphia: Westminster Press, 1947.

O'Collins, Gerald. "Karl Barth on Christ's Resurrection." *Scottish Journal of Theology* 26 (1973), pp. 85-99.

Phillips, John A. *Christ for Us in the Theology of Dietrich Bonhoeffer*. New York: Harper & Row, 1967.

Routley, Erik. *The Man for Others*. New York: Oxford University Press, 1964.

Thompson, John. *Christ in Perspective. Christological Perspectives in the Theology of Karl Barth*. Grand Rapids, MI: Wm. B. Eerdmans Publishing Co., 1974.

Tillich, Paul. *Systematic Theology II. Existence and the Christ*. Chicago: University of Chicago Press, 1957.

Waldrop, Charles T. *Karl Barth's Christology. Its Basic Alexandrian Character*. Berlin: Mouton Publishers, 1984.

54
Contemporary Christologies: Process Theologians

Barnhart, J.E. "Incarnation and Process Philosophy." *Religious Studies* 2 (1967), pp. 225-232.

* Griffin, David R. *A Process Christology.* Philadelphia: The Westminster Press, 1973.

Pittenger, W. Norman. *Christology Reconsidered.* London: SCM Press, 1970.

_____. *The Word Incarnate. A Study of the Doctrine of the Person of Christ.* New York: Harper & Brothers, 1959.

Pregeant, Russell. *Christology Beyond Dogma. Matthew's Christ In Process Hermeneutic.* Philadelphia: Fortress Press, 1978.

Weinandy, Thomas G. *Does God Change? The Word's Becoming in the Incarnation.* Still River, MA: St. Bede's Publications, 1985.

55
Contemporary Christologies: Teilhard de Chardin

Allegra, Gabriel M. *My Conversations with Teilhard de Chardin on the Primacy of Christ—Peking, 1942-45.* B.M. Bonsea, trans. Chicago: Franciscan Herald Press, 1971.

Bravo, Francesco. *Christ in the Thought of Teilhard de Chardin.* C.B. Larme, trans. Notre Dame, IN: University of Notre Dame Press, 1967.

Faricy, Robert. "Teilhard de Chardin's Spirituality of the Cross." *Horizons* 3 (1976), pp. 1-15.

Hale, Robert. *Christ and the Universe. Teilhard de Chardin and the Cosmos.* Chicago: Franciscan Herald Press, 1973.

Maloney, George A. *The Cosmic Christ. From Paul to Teilhard.* New York: Sheed & Ward, 1968.

Meilach, Michael D. *From Order to Omega.* Chicago: Franciscan Herald Press, 1967.

* Mooney, Christopher F. *Teilhard de Chardin and the Mystery of Christ.* New York: Harper & Row, 1966.

56
Christology and Anti-Semitism

Borowitz, Eugene. "Anti-Semitism and the Christologies of Barth, Berkouwer and Pannenberg." *Dialog* 16 (1977), pp. 38-41.

Flannery, Edward H. "Jesus, Israel and Christian Renewal." *Journal of Ecumenical Studies* 9 (1972), pp. 74-93.

Isaac, Jules. *Jesus and Israel*. C.H. Bishop, ed. S. Gran, trans. New York: Holt, Rinehart and Winston, 1971.

Kung, Hans, and Lapide, Pinchas. "Is Jesus a Bond or a Barrier? A Jewish-Christian Dialogue." *Journal of Ecumenical Studies* 14 (1977), pp. 466-483.

McGarry, Michael B *Christology After Auschwitz*. New York: Paulist Press, 1977.

Munck, Johannes. *Christ and Israel. An Interpretation of Romans 9-11*. Foreword by K. Stendahl, I. Nixon, trans. Philadelphia: Fortress Press, 1967.

Parkes, J. *Judaism and Christianity*. Chicago: University of Chicago Press, 1948.

_____ *The Foundations of Judaism and Christianity*. London: Valentine, Mitchell, 1960.

* Pawlikowski, John T. *Christ in the Light of the Christian-Jewish Dialogue*. New York: Paulist Press, 1982.

Rylaarsdam, J. Coert. "Jewish-Christian Relationship. The Two Covenants and the Dilemma of Christology." *Journal of Ecumenical Studies* 9 (1972), pp. 249-270.

Sandmel, Samuel. *Anti-Semitism in the New Testament?* Philadelphia: Fortress Press, 1978.

Sloyan, Gerard S. *Is Christ the End of the Law?* Philadelphia: The Westminster Press, 1978.

57
Christology And Ethics

* Driver, Tom F. *Christ in a Changing World. Toward an Ethical Christology.* New York: Crossroad Publishing Co., 1981.

* Gustafson, James M. *Christ and the Moral Life.* New York: Harper & Row, 1968.

Hiers, Richard H. *Jesus and Ethics. Four Interpretations.* Philadelphia: The Westminster Press, 1968.

Perkins, Pheme. *Love Commands in the New Testament.* New York: Paulist Press, 1982.

Ringe, Sharon H. *Jesus, Liberation and the Biblical Jubilee.* Philadelphia: Fortress Press, 1985.

Sanders, James A. "Torah and Christ." *Interpretation* 29 (1975), pp. 372-390.

58
The Uniqueness And Finality
Of Christ

Cook, Michael L. *The Jesus of Faith. A Study in Christology.* New York: Paulist Press, 1981.

Cullmann, Oscar. "The Unique Character of the Redemptive Epochs." *Christ in Time*, Philadelphia: The Westminster Press, 1964, pp. 119-174.

Hellwig, Monika K. "The Uniqueness of Jesus in Christian Tradition." *Does Jesus Make a Difference?* ed. by Thomas M. McFadden. New York: The Seabury Press, 1974, pp. 81-98.

Kirkpatrick, Dow, ed. *The Finality of Christ.* Nashville, TN: Abingdon Press, 1966.

Rahner, Karl. "The Death of Jesus and the Closure of Revelation." *Theological Investigations*, XVIII, trans. by E. Quinn. New York: Crossroad, 1983, pp. 132-142.

_____ "The One Christ and the Universality of Salvation." *Theological Investigations*, XVI, trans. by D. Morland. New York: Crossroad, 1982 reprint; first ET 1979, pp. 199-224.

Riedlinger, Helmut. "The Universal Kingship of Christ." *Who is Jesus of Nazareth?*, ed. by E. Schillebeeckx et al. New York: Paulist Press, 1965, pp. 107-127.

Sloyan, Gerard S. *Is Christ the End of the Law?* Philadelphia: The Westminster Press, 1978.

Vinay, Samuel and Sugden, Chris, eds. *Sharing Jesus in the Two Thirds World. Evangelical Christologies of Poverty, Powerlessness and Pluralism.* Grand Rapids, MI: Wm. B. Eerdmans, 1983.

59
Christ and Culture

Braaten, Carl E. *Christ and Counter-Christ. Apocalyptic Themes in Theology and Culture*. Philadelphia: Fortress Press, 1972.

Dias de Araugo, Joao. "Images of Jesus in the Culture of the Brasilian People." *Faces of Jesus*, ed. by J. Miguez-Bonino. Maryknoll, NY: Orbis Books, 1984, pp. 30-38.

Gunton, Colin E. *Yesterday & Today. A Study of Continuities in Christology*. Grand Rapids, MI: Wm B. Eerdmans Publishing Co., 1983.

* Niebuhr, H. Richard. *Christ and Culture*. New York: Harper & Row, 1951.

Pelikan, Jaroslav. *Jesus through the Centuries. His Place in the History of Culture*. New Haven: Yale University Press, 1985.

* White, Leland Jennings. *Christ and the Christian Movment. Jesus in the New Testament, the Creeds and Modern Theology*. New York: Alba House, 1985.

60
Political Issues In Christology

Bammel, Ernst. "The Revolution Theory from Reimarus to Brandon." *Jesus and the Politics of His Day*, ed. by E. Bammel & C.F.D. Moule. New York: Cambridge University Press, 1984, pp. 11-68.

* _____, and Moule, C.F.D., eds. *Jesus and the Politics of His Day*. New York: Cambridge University Press, 1984.

Brandon, S.G.F. *Jesus and the Zealots. A Study of the Political Factor in Primitive Christianity*. New York: Charles Scribner's Sons, 1967.

_____. "'Jesus and the Zealots.' A Correction." *New Testament Studies* 17 (1971), p. 453.

_____ *The Trial of Jesus of Nazareth*. New York: Stein and Day, 1968.

Cassidy, Richard J. *Jesus, Politics, and Society. A Study of Luke's Gospel*. Maryknoll, NY: Orbis Books, 1978.

* Cullmann, Oscar. *Jesus and the Revolutionaries*. New York: Harper & Row, 1970.

Derrett, J. Duncan M. "Luke's Perspective on Tribute to Caesar." *Studies in the New Testament* Vol. 4. Leiden: E.J. Brill, 1986, pp. 196-206.

Edwards, G.R. *Jesus and the Politics of Violence*. New York: Harper & Row, 1972.

Galilea, Segundo. "Jesus' Attitude Towards Politics. Some Working Hypotheses." *Faces of Jesus*, ed. by J. Miguez-Bonino. Maryknoll, NY: Orbis Books, 1984, p. 93-101.

Hengel, Martin. *Christ and Power*. Philadelphia: Fortress Press, 1977.

_____ *Victory Over Violence*. E. David Green, trans. Philadelphia: Fortress Press, 1973.

_____ *Was Jesus a Revolutionary?* W. Klassen, trans. Philadelphia: Fortress Press, 1971.

Kautsky, Karl. *Foundations of Christianity*. Henry F. Mins, trans. New York: Russell & Russell, 1953 reprint; orig. ed. 1908.

Maccoby, H. *Revolution in Judaea. Jesus and the Jewish Resistance*. New York: Taplinger Publishing Co., 1980.

Matthews, Shailer. *Jesus on Social Institutions*. Philadelphia: Fortress Press, 1971 reprint; orig. ed. 1928.

Richardson, Alan. *The Political Christ*. Philadelphia: The Westminster Press, 1973.

Smart, James D. *The Quiet Revolution. The Radical Impact of Jesus on Men of His Time*. Philadelphia: The Westminster Press, 1969.

Wiederkehr, Dietrich. "'Son of God' and 'Sons of God'. The Social Relevance of the Christological Title." *Jesus, Son of God?* ed. by E. Schillebeeckx and J.-B. Metz. New York: The Seabury Press, 1982, pp. 17-22.

Yoder, John Howard. *The Politics of Jesus*. Grand Rapids, MI: Wm. B. Eerdmans Publishing Co., 1972.

61
Psychological Studies of Christ

Barclay, William. *The Mind of Jesus.* New York: Harper & Row, 1960.

Bernard, Henry Norris. *The Mental Characteristics of the Lord Jesus Christ.* London: James Nisbet & Co., 1888.

* Canale, Andrew. *Understanding the Human Jesus. A Journey in Scripture and Imagination.* Introduction by M. Kelsey. New York: Paulist Press, 1985.

Comblin, Joseph. *Jesus of Nazareth. Meditations on His Humanity.* C. Kabat, trans. Maryknoll, NY: Orbis Books, 1976.

Dolto, Francoise, and Severin, Gerard. *The Jesus of Psychoanalysis. A Freudian Interpretation of the Gospel.* H.R. Lane, trans. Garden City, NY: Doubleday, 1979.

Guardini, Romano. *The Humanity of Christ. Contributions to a Psychology of Jesus.* R. Walls, trans. New York: Pantheon Books/Random House, 1964.

Howes, Elizabeth Boyden. *Jesus' Answer to God.* San Francisco: Guild for Psychological Studies Publishing House, 1984.

Leslie, Robert C. *Jesus and Logotherapy. The Ministry of Jesus Interpreted through the Psychotherapy of Viktor Frankl.* Nashville, TN: Abingdon, 1965.

McKenna, David L. *The Jesus Model.* Waco, TX: Word Books, 1977.

Sanford, John A. *The Kingdom Within. A Study of the Inner Meaning of Jesus' Sayings.* Philadelphia: Lippincott, 1970.

Schweitzer, Albert. *The Psychiatric Study of Jesus. Exposition and Criticism.* Boston: Beacon Press, 1948.

Snell, James Howard. *A Study of the Relationship Between the Teachings of Jesus in the Book of Matthew and the Existentialist Psychology of Rollo May.* Ann Arbor, MI: University Microfilms, 1978.

62
Comparative Religious Studies of Christ

Anderson, Gerald, and Stransky, Thomas F., eds. *Christ's Lordship and Religious Pluralism*. Maryknoll, NY: Orbis Books, 1983.

Borsch, Frederick Houk. *The Christian and the Gnostic Son of Man*. Napierville, IL: Alec R. Allenson, 1970.

Carmody, James H. "Towards a Comparative Christology." *Horizons* 1 (1974), pp. 15-33.

Carmody, John. "A Next Step for Catholic Theology." *Theology Today* 32 (1976), pp. 371-381.

Davis, Charles. *Christ and the World Religions*. New York: Herder and Herder, 1971.

Miller, David L. *Christs. Meditations on Archetypal Images in Christian Theology*. New York: The Seabury Press, 1981.

Pannikar, R. *The Unknown Christ of Hinduism*. Revised Ed. Maryknoll, NY: Orbis Books, 1980.

Parrinder, Geoffrey. *Avatar and Incarnation*. London: Faber & Faber, 1970.

Pieris, Aloysius. "Speaking of the Son of God in Non-Christian Cultures, e.g., in Asia." *Jesus, Son of God?* ed. by E. Schillebeeckx and J.-B. Metz. New York: The Seabury Press, 1982, pp. 65-70.

Rahner, Karl. "Jesus Christ in the Non-Christian Religions." *Theological Investigations*, XVII, trans. by M. Kohl. New York: Crossroad, 1981, pp. 39-50.

——————— "Oneness and Threefoldness of God in Discussion with Islam." *Theological Investigations*, XVIII, trans. by E. Quinn. New York: Crossroad, 1983, pp. 105-121.

* Richard, Lucien. *What Are They Saying About Christ and World Religions?* New York: Paulist Press, 1981.

Rupp, G. *Christologies and Cultures. Toward a Typology of Religious World Views.* The Hague: Mouton & Co., 1974.

Singh, Surjit. *Christology and Personality.* Philadelphia: The Westminster Press, 1966.

Song, Choan Seng. "The Role of Christology in the Christian Encounter with Eastern Religions." *Christ and the Younger Churches*, ed. by George F. Vicedom. London: SPCK, 1972, pp. 68-83.

63
Various Topics

Farmer, William R. *Jesus and The Gospel.* Philadelphia: Fortress Press, 1982.

Feuillet, Andre. *The Priesthood of Christ and His Ministers.* Garden City, NY: Doubleday & Co., 1975.

Riches, J.K. "What is a Christocentric Theology?" *Christ Faith and History,* ed. by S. W. Sykes and J.P. Clayton. New York: Cambridge University Press, 1972, pp. 223-238.

Smith, Jerome. *A Priest Forever. Typology and Eschatology in Hebrews.* London: Sheed & Ward, 1969.

Smith, Morton. *Jesus the Magician.* New York: Harper & Row, 1978.

Stagg, E. & F. *Women in the World of Jesus.* Philadelphia: The Westminster Press, 1978.

Stanley, David M. *Jesus in Gethsemane.* New York: Paulist Press, 1980.

TeSelle, Eugene. *Christ in Context. Divine Purpose and Human Possibility.* Philadelphia: Fortress Press, 1975.

Vogtle, Anton. "The Miracles of Jesus Against their Contemporary Background." *Jesus in His Time,* ed. by H.

J. Schultz. Philadelphia: Fortress Press, 1971, pp. 96-105.

Wahlberg, Rachel Conrad. *Jesus According to a Woman.* New York: Paulist Press, 1975.

Index

Index